M000290163

What's Funny About Dementia? Laugh To Keep From Crying Reviews

Jataun J. Rollins has accomplished a literary triumph with her book, *What's Funny About Dementia? Laugh to Keep from Crying*. Rollins' roles of caregiver for her grandmother and respite provider for her grandfather are warmly presented through a series of vignettes that reveal the family's journey through a loved one's stages of Alzheimer's disease. The author conveys a down-to-earth, authentically African American cultural experience to which people of any race, ethnicity or educational level can relate and/or appreciate. Her caregiving and social work background lend credence to the resources that Rollins provides in the appendix for caregivers and persons affected by dementia. I highly recommend this book to all families with elderly parents or grandparents, especially those who are caring for a loved one with Alzheimer's or other related dementia.

> Pauline Williams, Ph.D.
> Associate Professor, Illinois State University
> Producer/ Talk Show Host of "For All of My Sisters"

This book evoked so many emotions! I have cried from memories of my Mom's dementia and the common threads shared with dear 'Maggie.' I also laughed until I cried; especially the night they called 911 as Jataun and her granddad struggled to get Maggie to the hospital. I felt as if I were there and actually wanted to help in the struggle! She took the reader 'there'! ...The brutal honesty throughout this book tugged at my heart as I recounted incidents with my Mom's dementia.

> Debbie Mack, MLS
> Electronic Resource Coordinator
> Atlanta-Fulton Public Library System

I love your book so much, until it's difficult to expand on what chapters I like best. You are an excellent writer. The book is funny and exhilarating. It seems every chapter gave me a good laugh. It was great you could laugh and cry at the same time. Your grandma was hilarious. If, you had not understood Dementia and Alzheimer's you would not have been able to be so understanding. In fact, you may have thought you were losing it! ...Again, the book is enlightening and your chapter titles are so appropriate. Even though it is a memoir and cathartic for you; it is my belief; that this book would be an excellent book for beginning social workers. They could learn a lot from your experience. It certainly would be beneficial and helpful to families as well.

> Ollie M. Knight, MSW/DHL
> Independent Consultant

I loved the book and can't wait to get my hard copies. It's an easy read and I laughed out loud and reminisced. This book is a "promise fulfilled and a woman well honored." I love the chapter reflections. They are rich and help to make this book a great text for various courses in social work including aging and diversity courses. ...The chapter reflections are powerful reminders of life lessons along with concrete information, suggestions and encouragement.

> Iris Carlton-LaNey, Ph.D.
> Berg-Beach Distinguished Professor of Community Social Work
> School of Social Work
> The University of North Carolina at Chapel Hill

I enjoyed reading the book immensely; it was a super easy read because you spoke so humanely & transparently about your family experience. Each chapter made me want to know & read more. I found great humor, but immensely identified with the challenges & burdens of the caregiver role that my mom and I played in my brother's care. I loved how you talked about granddad and shared his perspective; spoke and expressed his language & understanding of the disease because so many loved ones just don't get it. ... The appendix is great, full of resources & tools.

Lupeda Brown, LCSW
Maternal Child & Health Outreach
Lawndale Christian Health Center

What's Funny

About Dementia?

Laugh to Keep From Crying

A MEMOIR

Jataun J. Rollins, LCSW

Co-Author of U.G.L.Y. Uncovering God's Love For You

Jai Jai's Consulting & Publishing

Chicago

WHAT'S FUNNY ABOUT DEMENTIA? Laugh to Keep From Crying.
Copyright © 2018 by Jataun J. Rollins. First Edition, 2018.

Published by Jai Jai's Consulting & Publishing
ISBN 978-0-999837900
Library of Congress Control Number 2018902704

All rights reserved. No part of this book may be used, reproduced or transmitted in any form or by any means, electronic or mechanical, including photocopying, recording or by any information storage and retrieval system, without the written permission of the copyright owner, the author and the publisher of the book, except for the inclusion of brief quotations in a critical article or review, magazine, newspaper or for broadcast.

For further information please contact:

Jai Jai's Consulting & Publishing
Jataun J. Rollins
1921 Ridge Road, #753
Homewood, IL 60430

To ensure privacy, some names have been changed.

This publication is designed to provide a firsthand account of caregiving and various ways of coping with caregiving responsibilities. The publisher and author desire for the reader to understand that the reader should seek professional expert assistance in the care of those with dementia and other related diseases specific to their circumstances.

PROJECT CREDITS

Book Cover Design: fiverr

Editor: Jataun J. Rollins

Author Photograph: Dr. Obari A. Cartman

Front Cover Photograph: Jataun J. Rollins

Back Cover Author's Make-up Artist: Joélle Rollins-Kent

Photograph Collections: Barbara Rollins, Jackie McNeal, Artra Nell Mosley, Marcelle Ferguson and Author

PRINTED IN THE UNITED STATES OF AMERICA

For Grandma Maggie and Granddaddy Booker T.,

May your journey with Alzheimer's change the lives of families who

battle dementia around the world!

"A merry heart does good, like medicine, but a broken spirit dries the bones."

Proverbs 17:22 (New King James Version)

♥ Contents ♥

♥ Dedication ♥

This book is lovingly dedicated to my mom, the memory of my maternal grandparents and my best friend, all special to me who helped me understand my purpose. They are my inspiration to help give voice to all those individuals and families impacted by Alzheimer's and to prayerfully lift the spirits of those who walk or have walked in my caregiving shoes.

Barbara Jean Rollins, my mom, survives them all as the ultimate caretaker who embraced her role having bonded more with her mother as her caregiver. She made many sacrifices to help her mom live her best life.

Maggie Passmore, affectionately known as Grandma to many, was a rock of salvation all the days of my life.

My grandfather, *Booker T. Passmore*, who like many spouses, sojourned through the agony of watching his wife of sixty-four years grapple with Alzheimer's holding onto hope that Grandma would get better.

My best friend, *Wanda Renee Williams*, was the most supportive of any of my relationships I had over the years--- loving, laughing and caring helping to keep me sane. She was also my memory; a lot of the other stories of my life departed with her, two months prior to the deaths of both my grandparents. She would joke that Grandma and Granddaddy would outlive us all--it would become her painful truth.

♥ Foreword ♥

Every caretaker has to find his or her path to peace. As a son who is currently providing care, it has been easier for me to care for an *imposter* in order to preserve the memory of my real mom, to distinguish her from the disease that destroyed her. So that it wouldn't destroy me. Before I read this book I would have said, "There is no way to prepare for the feeling of watching dementia slowly *destroy* someone you love." I wish I had a nicer word to use than *destroy*.

I didn't even know how much I decided to go about this alone. Not because there aren't people around that would love to talk to me, but because it hurts so much. My mother's dementia has been an ever-present blind spot, an evolving conundrum in my life. As difficult as it has been, it never had to be this lonely. I'm realizing now that there are others who share my pain.

I found myself so many times within Jataun's stories that I didn't realize that I didn't realize how lonely I have been. I like to know what I'm dealing with, so I can prepare to find my own peace. Jataun's approach is perfect for me, straight forward, hard truths, telling it like it is, yet full of compassion and wisdom.

Jataun and I are both in the helping profession; we're used to being the one people call for support. We're accustomed to having all the answers. Reading this book often felt like someone snuck into my heart and mind. The text explained so many feelings exactly as I experienced them. It is just now occurring to me that *I may have thought I was crazy*, that *no one would believe me*, or that *they would just offer one of those empty pleasantries that I'd have to respond to with a forced polite smirk*. The pleasantries were never helpful in my journey. People attempt to say nice things: *everything will be okay, she's still your mom, just a little different now*. I prefer reality to hope.

What Jataun offers instead is insightful tips and practical solutions. She really lays it all on the line. I'm simultaneously impressed and terrified by this book. I know how many internal mountains she had to climb, how many demons she had to wrestle with to present her journey with such clarity. I'm frightened though about how right she is, that now I have to face my own guilt and shame much more directly and it has to be done in community. I understand that I have to move beyond the isolation and draw upon the courage of Jataun's vulnerability, to share my journey ----at least with the people that love me. We often say things like "It takes a village."

We know intrinsically that family is important and we must love and care for one another. ***But what if the village is sick? What if the family has been systemically traumatized for generations?*** Then simple instructions like work together and support your family are rendered useless. Jataun takes the veil off her family, reveals them for all of us to see, not just for her own catharsis, but for all of us. This book offers us a guide, telling us not only to love and work with our family, but also showing us how. My mother would've loved this book. That thought makes me sad.

My mother's name is Carla. She is still alive, kinda. A few years ago during the stage of her dementia when I was still fighting to fix her we would spend a lot time in hospitals and I heard lots of comments about how rare it was to have a son stepping up to invest so much as a caretaker. For years, not being able to fix my mother was my greatest shame. Nothing made me feel more like a failure.

No one says that who knew her. Anyone that spent any time with her knew how much she loved her children, and how much she sacrificed for us. My mom was extraordinarily committed to her family. She raised us so well that I never think twice about doing anything in my power to make sure she is okay. My mother loved us very much; Ma gave so much to us that I think it broke her.

Before the dementia, Ma was very lively, fly, fun and energetic. She loved going to events, she was an avid fitness enthusiast. She took photos, drew, sewed clothes, wrote poems and was an amazing cook. She loved to travel, help others and was always looking for new adventures. She loved her family. Then signs of early onset frontal lobe dementia started showing around the time her husband, my father, drowned. Like Jataun's grandmother, she also had thyroid problems and diabetes. Beyond her seemingly odd, suffering from grief and stress, we didn't take her condition seriously until people in the community started to tell us they saw Ma and she didn't seem to recognize them. She was in her early 50's when we got an official diagnosis.

I still figured I just needed to move home to take all of her responsibilities away, manage the properties my dad left and get the house finances in order all while dealing with a court case started by three women my father cheated on my mother with so they can have access to the estate for their three children and let my mother just rest. I figured all she needed was some relief, but she only got worse. I tried everything I could. I took her to the psychiatrist who sent me to the neurologist who referred me to a psychiatrist. I took her to a Naprapath. I took her to a Yoruba priest, sacrificed a chicken and buried it in my backyard. Nothing worked. She just got worse. I'm still dealing with the shame of not being able to save her. Everybody won't have to go through this particular experience of caretaking this way, but everybody has a mother and a grandmother.

The revelations of *What's Funny About Dementia? Laugh to Keep From Crying* gives me some permission to not be so hard on myself. To remember that my mother would've wanted me to live my fullest life possible.

At some point, I gave up trying to fix my mom and decided to continue with my life and transition into managing mom's comfort. Now two of my other siblings and our uncles all share in the caretaking. It's still hard every day. I can barely look her in the eye. I still feel a lot of guilt for not taking better care of her teeth. I shudder to think of how embarrassed she would be with her appearance. I hope she isn't still in there somewhere with an awareness that it's me having to clean her sometimes.

I think we made it through the most difficult stage though, *wandering*. Ma was young so she was a flight risk for years. We lost her a few times. Now, she mostly sleeps and eats. My five year old son was in a room where I was describing Ma to some seventh grade boys. I encouraged them to appreciate their mothers now, and I described my mom as *zombie like*. I didn't think my son was paying attention until he asked me a few days later if grandma was a zombie. I felt terrible for putting that thought in his head and scrambled to fix it---probably not very successfully.

As much as my mother has become an emblem for me of slow death, the experience of being so close to it and her being my literal source of existence, forces me to reframe my focus on living life more vigorously. Caring for Ma has left me with urgency to more fully live life and appreciate the simple things. I kiss my sons more than I probably would have otherwise. I eat more ice cream. I see more live music. I spend more time on the lakefront. I live twice as hard, on my mother's behalf, in my mother's honor.

The themes Jataun explores are much more universal than any specific medical condition. What Jataun gives us is a testament to family. It's a love letter to God. It's a story about sorrow and joy, managing through adversity, overcoming unimaginable life challenges. Along the way, she teaches us how to love ourselves in the meantime. She shows us how to be the medicine we need for ourselves, and how to recruit support when the rainbow isn't enough.

Jataun reminds me of what I already know about Black people and surviving memory loss: we are still who we are regardless and our mothers' mothers will live on through the smiles of our grandchildren. Times have been hard before, but we just have to continue to press on. I am confident that you will now be as enriched, encouraged and inspired as I was by reading the marvelous tales of joy, laughter and struggle of Jataun and her beautiful family in *What's Funny About Dementia: Laugh to Keep From Crying*.

-Dr. Obari Cartman

♥ About the Author ♥

Jataun J. Rollins is a licensed clinical social worker raised on Chicago's south side by her mother, Barbara, who modeled resiliency and the ability to overcome barriers as a strong, single parent that birthed compassion into her spirit. Her father, Theodore, is the other source of motivation for her life's work and fueled her passion to help oppressed, children and families.

Jataun began her career in social services in the early nineties working with disabled individuals. From there, she endeavored to affect positive changes within the field of child welfare at the *Illinois Department of Children and Family Services* worked in a number of positions from working on the front line as an investigator to an Associate Deputy over several units and programs. She worked on a variety of services at Children's Memorial Hospital and Interfaith House, a homeless shelter on Chicago's Westside. She was also an adjunct faculty member of *Northeastern Illinois University* and *Chicago State University* in their social work departments.

Ms. Rollins, a member of *Trinity United Church of Christ* since 1997, has participated in several ministries over the years. She is an active member of the *National Association of Black Social Workers* (NABSW), the local *Chicago ABSW* where she served as Chapter President from 2012-2016. She also holds a position on the board of *Christian Community Health Center*.

Her specialties are public speaking; consultation on all things child welfare; personal, organizational, professional development; workshops on blended families, hip hop music and the intergenerational connection, fatherhood; issues of aging; adolescent, individual and marital therapy and genealogy. Her favorite pastimes are road trips with her children, playing Scrabble with her daughter and crafting.

This is the author's second book project as she co-authored the book entitled *U.G.L.Y. Uncovering God's Love for You* with eight other amazing women who share their triumph over adverse life experiences held together by their faith and the acquisition of freedom through forgiveness!

Readers can look forward to upcoming book projects on issues of dementia, caregiving, parenthood, grief, issues relating to child welfare and fiction.

♥ What's Funny About Dementia? 1 ♥

Through humor, you can soften some of the worst blows that life delivers. And once you find laughter, no matter how painful your situation might be, you can survive it.

Bill Cosby

This quote reigned so true for me, keeping me sane while battling a disease that was utterly beyond my educated understanding. Is there anything funny about dementia? It depends on the minute, the day, the latest episode, how sleep deprived you are and who you ask. How can you as the caregiver or the families you work with find humor in murky water one day, clear the next and a hurricane on the horizon to be clear again? It is an emotional journey that will test even the most patient of people.

For years, I facilitated a workshop entitled, *"What's Funny About Dementia? Caregiving and Coping with Stress"* and the results are the same. I am usually approached afterwards with gratitude for sharing Grandma's story, saying what participants wish they could say aloud or how they identify with my characterizations of family situations.

Many caregivers I have interviewed or met tell me two things: ***If it wasn't for the Lord...*** or *I had to laugh to keep from crying.* Stress can debilitate you or it can kill you; especially, if you are a caregiver, you know the physical and emotional responses that your body goes through. You have to learn to cope which is a means to successfully adapt to the issues you face. It was cathartic for me to find the funny or risk my own health with the demands of my day to day responsibility. Loretta Veney, author of *Being My Mom's Mom* simply says, "You have to find the joy in the little things."[1] That point is key! I eventually learned to be in charge of my well-being.

Laughter is a natural pain killer due to the endorphins that are released in your body. It can lower serum cortisol levels, increase natural killer cells that fight off infection and it is a natural coping or defense mechanism. [2] According to Dr. Yip, humor used properly lightens pressure, revives hope, heals, strengthens and increases endurance.[3] My experience taught me to address my needs as a caregiver first; find a safe place/person to share my experience; ensure the humor is not mean spirited, disrespectful or embarrassing to the survivor and alter your lens to see the absurd, off beat and funny experiences you encounter. You don't have to be so serious.

Adult children of survivors of dementia have added levels of uncertainty that accompany the journey with Alzheimer's. They worry about financial costs, complex treatment decisions, prognosis of any other medical treatments, conflict between siblings, conflict with the survivor's spouse/partner relating to

[1]Veney, L. (2013). *Being My Mom's Mom.* West Conshohocken, PA: Infinity.

[2]Thorson, J. Powell, F. Sarmany-Schuller, I. & Hampes, W. (1997). Psychological Health and Sense of Humor. *Journal of Clinical Psychology.* 53, 605-619.

[3]Yip, K. (2003). The relief of a caregiver's burden through guided imagery, role playing, humor, paradoxical intervention. *American Journal of Psychotherapy.* 57, 109-120.

caregiving decisions and the struggle with acceptance or denial of the dementia diagnosis.[4] These matters are difficult enough for those who step in to assist family members who have other health concerns without dementia. I am a strong advocate for family meetings, organizing tasks and documenting these personal experiences. The weight of it is so heavy that sometimes things get clouded; time gets blurred in your effort to communicate progression of the disease to a healthcare provider or ancillary supports who rely on this information.

It is highly encouraged that you journal, use a voice recorder, a note taking app on your smartphone or record your experiences on a digital recorder. Trust me, you will not likely find the funny in the things you experience in the moment, but after time passes and the emotions of it die down you may see the humor in it. Making sense of it all through writing can significantly aid you in your understanding. Prayers and intercessory prayer give you hope that things will get better in context of you managing your journey with Alzheimer's.

Be hopeful, live in the moment, focus on what the survivor needs at the time and recognize that there is a person inside. Do this in tandem with taking care of yourself as the caregiver. And remember this wonderful quote by Mary Pettibone Poole who said, *"He who laughs, lasts."* Survivors count on the caregivers to last, their well-being depends on it.

[4]Stone, A. & Jones, C. (2009). Sources of uncertainty: Experiences of alzheimer's disease. *Issues in Mental Health Nursing.* 30, 677-686.

♥ Introduction 2 ♥

Being a social worker by profession, the natural inclination for the touchy feely, rational understanding of Alzheimer's escaped me in the throes of our family's personal dilemma. It would be the norm to throw formal education out the window during the time I spent as Grandma's caregiver. I seemed to be in a state of constant crisis just trying to live. A small faction of my family probably cared less about my credentials and often dismissed my recommendations along the way. The disease taunted us with good days, bad days and days that we'd much rather forget altogether. Our hopes would get high, we'd thank God that it hadn't gotten worse and in the next five minutes of that thought we'd retract that statement. My then fifteen-year old daughter, Joélle, said it best after a visit at our grandparents, *"Grandma seems like she's getting better, but she's not."*

Alzheimer's erroneously known by some as "old timers" and "all timers" disease," alters the essence of the person outwardly while tangles of plaque corrupt the brain's capacity to remember. The scariest part, for me, is the unknown day to day experiences you can expect to face in any given moment. *No day is ever the same.*

Caregiving is a tremendous responsibility for someone entrusted to provide for the complete well-being of another human being involves the mind, body, spirit, financial, environmental, relational and social engagement. For example, the caregiver makes the decision about how often one should bathe, decide what and when they eat, arrange for alternate care, transport them to medical appointments, share information, advocate on their behalf and keep them engaged in some way. At least, that's how it typically occurs when one doesn't have a partner or spouse. Now fold a spouse or partner, the other in the mix and you have a soap opera in the making trying to navigate their opinions, run of the household and the plan of care. The "other" can be demanding and see the caregiver as an intruder trying to "take over their home." Or they may feel the need to let it be known who is in charge. Or they may fully rely on the caregiver for a number of things and essentially have them on speed dial all times of the day or night.

An added amount of stress is inevitable if you do not take the time to make the "other" feel included and validate their input as valuable. Ignoring family dynamics is a quick way to get put out or cussed out which happened to me more times than I care to admit. I'd show up like nothing ever happened and start all over again. Granddaddy knew how to push a button and lean on it. Sometimes I fell right into his madness, while other times I let it roll off my back like a duck. Holding grudges affected me physically and threw me off kilter, so I couldn't stay mad for long.

Caregiving can be an awesome, dynamic, life changing opportunity to not only learn more about the one you care for, but you may end up knowing the people around you and yourself better. There will be moments when one has to self-check, self-correct and take an introspective look at how to cope with the totality of stress embedded in the caregiving responsibilities. Whenever you as the caregiver feel alone carrying the weight of the world, get help. You can't do this by yourself without ramifications to your quality of life and your health.

Until you walk in the shoes of a caretaker for someone with Alzheimer's or other dementias, one cannot completely understand how overwhelming the responsibilities can be. You can only try to make an attempt to prepare for what it may do to your mind, heart and spirit. Be intentional, do what you can when you can without burning yourself out as it may leave you bitter.

Each chapter is set up with the author's narrative and ends with a reflection by the author. Please use the white space at the end of the chapters to reflect on your own experiences. Surely, there is a relatable experience you can recall, so that you might capture your own journey with dementia and share your experience. I hope each reading experience gives you a chuckle, a fresh thought about your own respective experience and solace in knowing you are not alone.

Prayerfully, you will gain peace in the midst of a storm. For those of you, who already know the degree of drama this disease can bring, look for a measure of hope that we might all be saved from it.

♥ Chapter Reflection ♥

Providing care for those impacted by Alzheimer's and other dementias requires the buy-in from everyone involved who can offer the best care possible as a team. Family members are not necessarily impressed with your credentials even if this is your area of expertise because they put you in a box of what role they have ascribed to you. Well, let me say mine did.

You don't own the disease or the person; endeavoring to own the disease or the person can isolate others from helping or give them an excuse not to assist. Another danger of taking ownership of Alzheimer's in the life of the one surviving the disease is "doing too much" and is a set up from the outset to be wearier and more fatigued than necessary. Make a way to connect with others, be it on the phone, social media or maybe a family dinner night to keep family and friends engaged with the caregiver and the person requiring care. It will definitely enhance their quality of life and yours. Expect the unexpected, roll with the punches and focus on the goal.

See the Appendix for activities that can engage family that even the youngest can help with the care of the survivor of Alzheimer's. If nothing else, varied participation creates normalcy and strengthens connections. Note: when all else fails there is something extremely magical about babies, children and pets with older individuals in general that creates a much friendlier, lighter environment.

PSALM 23: 1- 6 KJV

[1]A Psalm of David. The LORD is my shepherd; I shall not want. [2]He maketh me to lie down in green pastures: he leadeth me beside the still waters. [3]He restoreth my soul: he leadeth me in the paths of righteousness for his name's sake. [4]Yea, though I walk through the valley of the shadow of death, I will fear no evil: for thou art with me; thy rod and they staff they comfort me. *[5]Thou preparest a table before me in the presence of mine enemies: thou anointest my head with oil; my cup runneth over. [6]Surely goodness and mercy shall follow me all the days of my life: and I will dwell in the house of the LORD forever.*

My earliest memories of Grandma Maggie occurred before I could speak as a young child and were synonymous with warmth, comfort and love. Besides sitting at the breakfast table, the next best place to sit was on Grandma's cushy lap where she would envelope me with her full arms and plant a kiss on my head. That kind of love is immeasurable to me and makes the most poignant argument that the formative years of children are very impressionable. It was that display of love that prompted me without hesitation to care for her when she needed help.

I imagine that's why I've always taken to youngest children in the family to pay it forward what I received as a young child. My grandmother modeled for me several positive qualities one of which is that *to be in God's grace you must first love*, love all, including your friends and even your enemies. There should be no difference between them and those close to you. Prayer was her life.

Saturday nights and Sunday mornings, you'd find one of God's most devoted disciples studying her bible. She had to prepare her "Sunday lesson" dressed in her uniform: a full slip and a snap buttoned house dress. The smell of Grandma's breakfast always wafted over the morning dew wet cement scent. On Sundays, she would navigate the *Word* and breakfast with ease preparing an effortless meal of the creamiest grits oozing with butter, a pan of hot flaky homemade biscuits, crispy country bacon, scrambled eggs sometimes accompanied by the best salmon croquettes I have ever tasted in life and a cold tall jelly glass of orange juice. There was always a bowl of the largest fruit I ever saw from Granddaddy's shopping bounty. The roles were clear, evident who was who and who did what.

The opening passage of scripture embodies how Grandma lived life from the moment she embraced the Lord as her Savior, as I imagine, to the moment she took her last breath. I believe she's forever dwelling in the house of the Lord. She taught me this very early on as a child before I even knew how to speak. In her prior secular life, Grandma was a glitzy gal who would get dressed in her best

dresses and go out dancing with family. Then 1967 came; she had a new life and would raise her children, her children's children and their children in the church. Grandma was saved, a devoted Pentecostal servant for the Church of God in Christ, also known as COGIC.

It became the essence of how *"Sista Passmore"* would be remembered until the day of her homegoing. Grandma was the first individual to introduce me to God and modeled every day of her life, for as long as I can remember, what it meant to be in relationship with God. God never fails. I never connected Grandma to my roots in social work until this very moment on a brisk January night, in dim light tapping away about the story of her life reflecting on how she left her mark upon the world in such an awesome way.

As a God-fearing woman, she embraced the Bible as her "bread and butter." She emphatically told us this very point on a quite memorable family trip to Ray Charles' *Georgia*, in the summer of 2001. It was then she displayed many signs that she was transforming. She left her diabetes medication at home, regressed to acting like a three-year old child, was overly dramatic with the smallest of things and fasted from food & water on a long hot day. None of us knew at the time that her odd behavior was an indicator that her illness was already taking root in her mind.

This woman faithfully attended church all day Sunday, Tuesday and Friday nights; taught Sunday school and attended YPWW until one horrific day that changed her life forever as discussed in the chapter entitled *Diabetic Coma Bypass*. After that unforgettable night, most days Grandma seemed to be a shell where a once lively spirit dwelled. I become teary eyed from time to time when I think of all the things that occurred from the time I noticed a change in her to experiencing the worst of the worst moments feeling like an idle, powerless bystander watching Grandma slowly die—for years and years. My narrative would later change because Grandma would push past Alzheimer's a lot and have beautiful lucid moments clapping, singing, dancing, laughing and crying just as one would if they weren't "sick." In fact, *she wasn't dying; she was living and surviving in spite of her illness.*

A few short years later, Grandma's life dramatically changed the day her blood glucose level read over 600. By nightfall, she cycled through several episodes of crying and laughing maniacally within seconds of each other. She was hospitalized; she would never attend church alive after that fateful February night in 2003. She suffered several mini strokes called transient ischemic attacks when her "sugar" levels spiked high.

I moved, willingly, into Grandma's home with two young children, my then two year old son and nine year old daughter, in an effort to right my inability to advocate for my great grandmother, Big Ma, who suffered from dementia when I

11

was an adolescent. They didn't call it Alzheimer's back then. Admittedly for selfish reasons because of *Big Mama*, I wanted Grandma to live a long life in the best health she could have for as long as she had breath. It was important to me that I made an effort to do something.

My life was built on fixing people, situations and things yet I was rendered helpless in a few situations over time. I attempted to pay her back for all she had done for me since I was a child as there is no value I can put on a lifetime of love and commitment. She deserved to live with love, support and with integrity, just as she had treated countless members of her church and family over the years. If she wasn't on the bus, my grandfather was dropping her off for her "sick and shut in" rounds.

Grandma was a breast cancer survivor since 1985, a diabetic and newly diagnosed in 2003 with a thyroid condition all of which add to the accounts on the following pages. If nothing else, her resiliency, undying faith and love of God kept her here for the many years she lived. Our family was blessed to have been in her midst because of her faith. This book celebrates Grandma as the person I once knew and "Sick Grandma" which was the easiest way to explain Grandma's diagnosis to my youngest child. I missed the nuances of her *sugar pop sweet on top pudding pop* Grandma face. I miss Grandma's sugar, a light kiss on the cheek or the forehead with the warmest of embraces was the best.

In her final years when she no longer spoke (a form of aphasia), I would promise her that I was going to tell her story to as many people as I could so that they might be comforted that they were not alone and give them tips on what we learned over time through trial and error. I can still retreat to my "happy place" honoring her in all she did because she was there for me.

Grandma lost her ability to cook; she would forget that she had food on the stove. She'd go sit down on the couch to watch her western shows and get lost in her world forgetting she had something on the stove. Eventually, hot dogs and polish sausages were banned from the home because it was a quick and easy snack for her and the kids with just as much ease to become a threat to safety. Those two food items sparked her memory to cook which resulted in many pot burnings. It took longer than it should have for family members to understand the gravity of this and to stop buying them. It was a hard lesson learned that thankfully brought her the 24 hour supervision she needed.

This book was not written to make a mockery of this disease or disparage the life of my grandmother and my family. I imagine some family members will have some hurt feelings. *What's Funny About Dementia?* is more about those who try to manage the life of survivors today. I wrote it, so other people who get inducted into the sorority or fraternity of caregivers could be more reflective on their personal journey and change their narrative to optimism. *Writing my experiences was one of the things I had to do. The other was laugh to keep from crying.* Through this manner of coping I was able to reframe my experiences more positively.

13

Journaling was cathartic and natural for me since I had been writing as a teen. I began to compile many stories, funny and not so funny and retell them at work, at home and to anyone who would listen. My friends would make requests for their favorite stories. Usually what I captured in my journal was never funny in the moment, but a week or two later you couldn't tell me I wasn't living a Tyler Perry sitcom. I could find the humor in my encounters with Alzheimer's because it was natural to our family to use it as a coping mechanism.

A number of days, I felt like I was losing my mind, so laughing at myself or the madness of the situation became one of my lifelines. I became depressed weighing 240 pounds on a small 5'7" frame with *Mr. Osteoarthritis* taking refuge in my knees. My face was unrecognizable to even myself and I was uncomfortable in my skin. The only time I had to myself was Thursday nights for one hour when the world stopped, so I could get lost in my favorite reality show, *Survivor*. Everybody knew I shut it down from 7 to 8 pm and nothing short of life threatening activity would garner my attention off television. My regimen was mundane and tiring as I lived three shifts. Work. Home. Cook. Eat. Watch her. Watch the kids. Clean. Help. Repeat.

♥ Chapter Reflection ♥

The memories of the people we once knew who survive this journey with Alzheimer's and other dementias have laid a foundation for us to be intentional in tapping into the essence of their being. **We need to celebrate the ways in which the survivor added quality to our life; memory is so overrated because it is inevitable that it will be lost, so just focus on what abilities they still possess rather than lament over what was and will never be again.**

The emphasis we place on memory as a society undercuts the capacity of the survivor and the potential for sustainable relationship and meaningful engagement in the life they have left to live. We can remember the survivor we once knew via photos, videos, heirlooms, recipes, traditions, values and if they are still with us, the way they make you feel. If you are experiencing the early stages of the disease with them, consider building in some time that you listen to their narratives and recording or documenting family connections, family tales and the most mundane. **There is still time to make memories.**

After Grandma died I wished I would have talked to her more about her life growing up. I wish I wrote down all her recipes and watched her make my favorites. There are so many unanswered questions now that she is gone and if I knew then what I know now, I would have been more attentive and intentional on capturing my legacy. So now, my Great Aunt Artra Nell, her only living sibling at ninety-two years old is now my window to Grandma via her memories which is just as precious. **Take nothing for granted—ever!**

♥ Eerily Familiar   4 ♥

Grandma was very good at navigating public transportation. Family and friends for years would always inform me that they saw Grandma and my daughter, Joélle on somebody's bus stop or on their way somewhere on the bus.

In time, Grandma would get lost and come home hours later because she *"got turned around."* Grandma was the *Queen of Sick and Shut In* for quite a few years visiting the entire congregation of her church as needed. She navigated the streets only armed with the *Word of God,* morning, noon or night with good cheer to bring an encouraging word to those who fell ill. If it was too late in the evening, my granddaddy was just a phone call away as her personal Uber.

Big Mama lived a long time too ---compounded with many years of limited memory. She lived alone in a family occupied building as far as I can remember. She was very organized, strong willed and set in her ways. I couldn't understand why she was allowed to live alone when it seemed obvious to me in my youth that something was different and changing in her. I guess I have always been observant of people. The food *Big Mama* used to cook well, didn't taste the same.

It tasted like the ingredients were not all making it into the recipe. She seemed to grow thinner each time I saw her, the smell of her house changed and her appearance too. *Big Mama* had been a very well dressed, put together woman who was always stylish. I remember she always had this thing about taking pictures—she didn't want to unless her hair was done or unless she had on one of her wigs. I don't have very many pictures in later years because of her desire not to be photographed.

Then the day soon came when she forgot my name and who I was. I was no longer *Nae Nae*. I would walk into a room and *Big Mama* didn't bat an eyelash my way with no greeting of any kind. No one explained what was going on to me, so I internalized it and was hurt to my core and angry. Angry with her for not remembering me, angry for feeling no one was doing anything to stop the inevitable and angry that I was losing someone I loved dearly. That period of adolescence when the world is about you ensconced by pure narcissism and her faded memory of me was crushing. There were feelings of emptiness as a youth watching, *Big Mama* transform.

According to Cousin Jackie, *Big Mama* complained about the heat not working and she once poured water in her electric heater which had to be taken away because she didn't realize the degree of danger she was in—doing that. She died when I was twenty-four years old and that was a significant loss in my life.

Five generations alive and engaged with one another was a blessing. Thankfully, my daughter accompanied Grandma on visits to the nursing home quite regularly toting fish and Dock Berry Shakes for *Big Mama* and got to experience her even though she was so young. Fortunately, my son and daughter would spend time up close and personal with their own great grandmother, Maggie, because she was an integral part of their development from the beginning.

A flashback if you will: The nursing facility where *Big Mama* died as a matter of protocol did not perform an autopsy at the time of her death because she died in a nursing care facility; therefore, her death was not an unusual circumstance. The chance to verify what I presumed to be Alzheimer's was shot down unless someone wanted to pay a few hundred dollars for an autopsy since at that time that was the only method of diagnosing Alzheimer's was in death. I didn't have the money to get closer to our family's truth and felt powerless. Damn it, if it didn't hit me again, the overwhelming feeling of powerlessness when I faced the truth that Grandma was sharing her mother's fate. The question, "Do we or do we not have a destiny date with Alzheimer's?" remained unanswered for about five more years until Grandma began dropping clues of her decline in health that we dismissed as an issue of age.

My Great Aunt Artra Nell and my Cousin Jackie recounted their most memorable moment that her grandmother, my great grandmother, Bettie Mack aka *Big Mama* also shared a knack for traveling on *Chicago Transit Authority* modes of transportation. Grandma preferred the bus, while *Big Mama* rode the el train and the bus to the western suburbs to do domestic work. Cousin Jackie recounted the story of *Big Mama's* last day of work. The last day of work would parallel Grandma's last days of church. *Big Mama* left for work as she normally did arriving in the western suburbs but went missing for several hours.

Cousin Jackie said she got anxious after a few hours noting that *Big Mama's* routine had been broken and it was not like her to be so late getting home from work. She sought the help of a family friend whom *Big Mama* entrusted with the number to her employer. Cousin Jackie pleaded for the friend to provide her with the number or to connect with the employer to which she did valuable hours later. According to her employers, *Big Mama* had been placed on the train at 1 pm earlier that day, it started to get dark and was about 8 pm before she arrived home.

Big Mama missed her stop several times and rode the el train from the south side of Chicago's end of the line to the North side of Chicago's end of the line before finally making it home on the bus. *Big Mama* was disoriented when Cousin Jackie saw her and she made an executive decision to call her employers and advise them her Grandma Bettie would not be returning to work anymore. *Big Mama* would later make her transition in March 1995 inside a nursing care facility. Grandma really wore her *Queen of Sick and Shut In* crown to the facility several times a week with Dock's fish and a shake in hand with Joélle in tow to see *Big Mama*. Who knew how eerily familiar their lives would be?

It would come to light that she suffered a series of mini strokes to the brain just as Grandma did in the day her life changed forever. While Grandma was nearing her big reveal that she had Alzheimer's, her brother, Uncle Jessie would die from complications of Alzheimer's as well.

Cousin Jackie said that *Big Mama's* late home arrival and not navigating her way home sooner was a clear sign for her that something was wrong. Grandma's getting *turned around* on public transportation became too frequent not to notice and she required the limo services of her husband more. A clear sign of their diminishing capacity to travel alone was compromised. That was the beginning.

♥ Chapter Reflection ♥

As a culture, we are dismissive at times of some behaviors displayed by our elders writing it off as part of the aging process. Those things that present as a clear and present danger usually signal in advance signs that there might be something wrong. Consider the multiplicity of occurrences and the weight of what happens in order to figure out a plan to minimize safety risks. A couple of plans should be in cue in the event the initial one doesn't work. The article by Stephen Matthews takes the focus off memory loss and the pre-dementia symptoms of behaviors and personality changes that signal the need for a screening.[5] If we had this thirty-five question behavioral change checklist years ago, we would have surely visited a physician sooner to see what treatment options were available. Technology and research is moving us much further now as our options would have been limited then.

Consistent contact with the survivor, their village of support combined with fluid,, transparent communication between family members, friends and social connections should be done strategically to assure the safety and well-being of your survivor with Alzheimer's. I would encourage the formulation of regular family meetings/dinners with an agenda of running concerns. A conference call can be held outside of the range of the survivor to discuss delicate issues. Great care has to be taken in the way these concerns are delivered. Messaging is everything, it can be upsetting if the conversation is centered on what someone is doing wrong.

Always start in a happy place with good stuff; chit chat on who is doing what, who is graduating or getting married, bought a home, got good grades, etc. Place yourself in the survivor's shoes and imagine if people called a meeting together to talk about you, some things personal and others not so much and you are convicted that there is something occurring with you. That would prove to be a dark place for you.

[5]Matthews, S. (2016, July 29). Will you get Alzheimer's? Answer these questions to find out: Checklist shows symptoms of disease before memory loss. from http://www.dailymail.co.uk/health/article-3714806/ Retrieved February 13, 2018

21

♥ First Signs 5 ♥

My immediate and extended family ventured on a trip to Georgia in hopes of meeting Granddaddy's Passmore side of the family back in August 2001. Grandma neglected to mention until hundreds of miles into our trip that she forgot to bring her diabetes medication for a trip that lasted several days. We drove in a caravan of cars making pit stops along the way. We began to pick up on some obvious clues that Grandma was not herself.

She became uncharacteristically combative, argumentative, belligerent and irrational. Personality changes are one of the signs of dementia. In the midst of travel, Grandma refused to use the restroom and declared that she was not hungry. She engaged in a biblical debate *with herself* proclaiming the Israelites would persevere and get the land. She held her bible in hand and announced very loudly to everyone in the SUV, "THIS IS MY BREAD AND BUTTER. IF I DON'T KNOW NOTHING ELSE, THIS I KNOW!!!!" This response came as a result of us having asked her to get out of the truck to use the bathroom and get something to eat. She refused. It wasn't rational, so we bought her some food anyway and she just about beat everybody eating because her body was craving nourishment after she deprived herself all day of food and water..

Later, we would learn that she was in the early stages of Alzheimer's during that trip. I hadn't figured it out sooner, since I did not make the connection to her mother's and brother's fight with dementia and Alzheimer's as one that would be Grandma's future battle. The few clues we did have signaled that Grandma could no longer live by herself anymore.

She was finally diagnosed with Alzheimer's in 2002, after several challenges with her primary doctor who insisted nothing was wrong with her. "Ohhhhhhh Maggie, it is nothing. I forget sometimes too," he would say. Her long time physician, let's just call him Dr. T because he ticked me off a number of times when I became her live in caregiver. I worked in a highly stressful position in child abuse investigations, cared for two young children, had my own medical issues and was very stressed with my new responsibilities as a result of not receiving help from my family.

I didn't have the energy to keep fighting with Dr. T. who provided medical care for both Grandma and Granddaddy for over 20 years. He was adamant that it was a natural part of the developmental milestone of an aging person. I begged to differ and kept pushing the issue, but they trusted him as if he was one of God's disciples because everything he said was the gospel truth. Granddaddy would get loud and say, "Dr. T saved my God damned life when I was about to die. You remember when you was crying and they wouldn't let you up to see me. And he saved your Grandmama too when she beat that cancer." Obviously, I couldn't win with this argument. I requested for Dr. T to complete a mini mental status exam anyway, and he refused. I surmise he didn't know what it was, so I sent the assessment tool with my grandma and sister to her appointment since I was working and couldn't attend.

It was not until I sought a second opinion from the University of Chicago where several family members were interviewed regarding our concerns. The university hospital confirmed what I already knew and had an awesome team of individuals to work with us. It was more expensive and expansive than the small neighborhood hospital where my grandparent's received care. Insurance coverage and co-pays ruled out Grandma's chance to get quality, personalized medical care at their facility, so back to the hood we went. We had to go back to Dr. T who was now forced to treat her, but he didn't think anything was wrong with her in the first place. That posed a serious problem for me. Before the family actually knew what was going on, Grandma was already dropping clues that life was changing for her and we didn't know how long a ride we were about to take journeying with her until the end for about fifteen years.

We would witness a change in every aspect of her life from the social to the physical to the spiritual. Everything. Everything. She cussed in the beginning, we would look at each other amused and ask ourselves if she just cussed. Over time she just stopped talking. Over the years, her hearty appetite never wavered in the midst of what I termed as her *long memory* of food indulgences. She loved to eat----everythang! Grandma was juicy weighing in over 200 pounds in the early 2000s. Sorry Grandma. We watched her girth go from full figured to a thin framed little woman weighing a mere 90 pounds.

Grandma knew how to praise the Lord; I imagine she prayed many a silent prayer even in the midst of losing some of her faculties. She made about fifteen sets of keys or more for the house and when pooled altogether she had over twenty pair of reading glasses. Grandma just kept on livin'. She was still faithful to God even though she was not able to attend church physically. She once said to me, "I don't know what's wrong with me. I got to get myself together and get back to church." All I could do was nod my head and say 'Yeah'.

♥ Chapter Reflection ♥

It seems we put off examinations that would help screen for Alzheimer's as if putting it off and not knowing will make it go away. We minimize, placate and ignore the signs as a means of coping with the gravity of losing someone to losing their memory. It is called denial. There are measures we should take in advance of not knowing if it will be us tapping in for the next battle.

I suggest individuals 50 and over (at the least) should consider long term insurance, ensure that living wills are in place, explore land trusts etc. as there could be a legal challenge in court if it is too late. A question of mental capacity could jeopardize plans of care for health and finances hence the famous line, "I, fill in the blanks, being of sound mind and body..."

Most importantly, be intentional about your own health whether you are reading this for yourself or passing it off to someone else. It starts with you to be your own lifeline journeying to wellness starting today to change y our eating habits, get some exercise in whatever way you can at least once a week. Sarah Knapton of The Telegraph simply stated *"...remember what is good for your heart is good for your head..."*

Maintain regular medical appointments to keep check on your health. Study findings indicate that African Americans are diagnosed with Alzheimer's at a higher rate than any other race/ethnicity. Hypertension, high cholesterol, poor circulation, stroke and diabetes significantly increases the risk of acquiring dementia. Although African Americans are most affected by this disease they are the least likely to participate in clinical trials for research.

I recall doing a presentation on caregiving and Alzheimer's for NASW-Illinois one year; a Rush University medical professional queried me afterwards if my family had considered participating in research in light of three instances of individuals having dementia. I also shared in my presentation that my uncle once told my mother that in his words, he believed he "has what Mama got" and of course, my mother conveniently has no recall of this.

I was excited about the opportunity to demystify our story with Alzheimer's and told my mom about Rush's ask for participation. I requested for my mom to talk it over with my aunt and uncle because one had to be at least 50 years old and willing to participate. I would ask her several more times for the next few months about her participation in a study and she said, "I'm not ready." I asked, "What does that mean and what does ready look like?" She said she didn't *know just that she "wasn't ready." If the question is posed of you, "Are you ready?"*

I reflected long and hard on "her readiness," really "our readiness" and how hard it would be to face a reality of whether Alzheimer's is inherited, familial or sporadic. I believe my mom's readiness included uncertainty about her future and caused a degree of anxiety and stress. I understand now that participating may leave you with some uncertainty as you don't know if you will receive a placebo or not. I can imagine the mental torment that might result as one questions what one can do about a disease that has no cure. Images of her and my mortality came to mind at the thought of the implications. More of us need to participate in research trials in order for us to get closer to a cure. Science is much further along today as there are an enormous amount of articles and books on the subject matter than when I started researching this in the early 2000s. Walking by faith for the things unseen gives us hope. We can now celebrate the long awaited breakthrough of the cure for sickle cell disease and pray that a cure for dementia is not too far off from discovery.

*For anyone with elderly parents, relatives or acquaintances, **recognize that it is not normal to have an abundance of coincidences and circumstances of unusual behavior that occurs repeatedly coupled with memory loss**. At first sign, take note and everyone else tied to that individual needs to keep notes as well. Put them altogether with conversation and you might have reason to request screening by your general practitioner.*

Grandma's "first signs" really were a wakeup call, in my opinion, that we, as a society, need to be more engaged in the healthcare management of the ones you love and be proactive: know their health status; appointment dates and times; know the name of the primary physician and know all prescribed and non-prescribed medications they take and who is the local pharmacist. Perhaps we could have reached out to Grandma's doctor, so that she could have gotten an emergency prescription of medication rather than wait it out all week.

In traveling with Grandma, a checklist of items before we left would have been helpful for the trip and to have kept her engaged in activities to reduce the angst of the "Are we there yet?" series of questions. It takes a village to work harmoniously together for better outcomes instead of being the lone man on the isle.

We hadn't been attentive that some things were changing with Grandma. Grandma provided child care for my son who was a few months old at the time. As a child welfare worker and investigator of abuse, my life revolved around

child victimization. She was my only and number one choice whom I trusted to care for my children. She declined initially as she told me she was getting too old, but I insisted I needed her, so she gave in. I was focused on my needs

and not hers; if there were signs I didn't want to see them. I was blinded by selfishness.

One day I felt compelled to go visit Grandma and the baby on my lunch break. This was a "*BUT GOD*" moment as it couldn't have been anything else, *BUT GOD* to order my steps that day. I was in grad school full time and usually stayed on campus because I was worried about losing a *good parking space* close to class. I had several conversations with Grandma about her locking the wrought iron storm door with the deadbolt, as it posed a fire hazard. I fussed and fussed with Grandma about the *what ifs* in case of an emergency if she couldn't find her key quickly. She would respond okay, not lock the doors for a little while and start locking it again. I thought she was just being belligerent or standing her ground expressing her need for independence. Then again, her reality was that she lived in a crime ridden neighborhood and her *long memory* remembered that, so she sided with safety. Dementia does that.

I got to Grandma's house and the storm door was locked. I didn't have my set of house keys. I rang the bell and rang the bell. No answer. I peered through the storm door as the entry door was cracked open. I saw smoke. I screamed and bammed on the door. Grandma was lying on the living room couch and I saw my baby on the couch in the dining room closest to the kitchen and I panicked. I frantically beat on the door and they still didn't move. My heart raced and I thought the worst. Grandma finally woke up and looked disoriented. She opened the door and I bolted past her to address the source of the smoke in the kitchen. Smoke billowed through the house. I ran back, got Jonathan and her out of the house onto the porch and I went back to vent the house. I thought one of my worst fears had come true.

Grandma started a pot on the stove, forgot and simply took a nap. She seemed oblivious to how serious this episode was and minimized it. She offered a series of apologies about how sorry she was promising it would never happen again. I cried and thanked God that I came home. I came home just in time. I dare not imagine what my life would have been like if my steps had not been ordered. There might not have been a book to tell about her journey. Once I calmed down, I told my mom what happened and she was alarmed, but life went on until the next thing happened. That was the day I knew I had to move in because Grandma couldn't live alone anymore. The *what if* finally happened! I finished school June 2001; I moved into Grandma's house by November of that year. She was happy for our company. I was glad for my children to grow up knowing and loving her just as I did as a child, but God was about to stretch me in ways unimaginable.

♥ Chapter Reflection ♥

The trick of Alzheimer's is its inconsistency. Patterns of behavior that individuals show are indicators and you cannot continue to dismiss what you are seeing. You might write off an event as a fluke, but then something else happens again and again. Grandma was capable of caring for herself more days than not. She still kept her routines as far as we knew. If we jumped in sooner we would have had a bigger fight on our hands because she wasn't ready. We would have had to deal with her being mad or her being dead because she might have done something that would have been harmful to her. **Trust your gut, recognize the signs and act on them with a plan. Safety trumps readiness any day.**

♥ Family Intervention Nite   7 ♥

Family Intervention night occurred on the season finale of Survivor in 2003. It was well known by all my friends and family to not call me during the seven o'clock hour when *my show* came on and surely this night was huge for me as this was the big closer for the season.

I found out that my Uncle had been taking advantage of Grandma again with his nonsense and my memory escapes me right now on what he did, but he likely pissed me off by eating my kids cereal again. Yes,-----you read right. Cereal! That's all I needed to *get it on and poppin'* with confrontation like I had done so many times before. Grandma would jump to my uncle's defense as usual and take his side no matter the issue. His reply was always, "Mama they lyin' on me!!!!" That was all she needed to hear to make her case to leave *him* alone.

Pulling up my sleeves making my way to engage in verbal warfare with someone who acted like he was twelve years old, I became Popeye that night because *that was all I could stand and I couldn't stand no more.* Yes, I should be ashamed. No, it was not my finest hour, but he could get you fired up instantly. He was a master of annoyance and a great wielder of bullsh*t. I'm trying to keep it clean should the kiddies read this book.

Anyway, I called up everybody including my mother, my aunt, my cousins young and old, my uncle and granddaddy to tell them it was time for an intervention. At first nobody came; not Granddaddy, my other uncle (no surprise there) and my mom were all no shows to the spectacular event that was about to begin. The folks trickled in as the night went on.

First, I outlined all the mess my uncle had been doing and then I gave an account of the way Grandma always fixed stuff for him. I talked about his continued drug use, his boldface lying to Grandma, his late-night runs beating on the windows at 1 and 2 am Grandma allowed him to come in late and sometimes with company. The kind of company you would see on the street walking in the night with eyes scouring the curb for drugs. I had a serious issue with this because prior to moving in, I set firm ground rules for my stay in order to protect my children from any illegal and unsavory behavior.

The family nodded their heads in disgust then folks started their *tell all session* on the wrongdoings they were aware of that my Uncle had done. He acted like a kid most days like when we were young children. We grew in maturation, but he didn't. I venture to use an old phrase in that my uncle acted "a lil touched." The conversation went from what he was doing at that point in time to what he did in the past including the distant past. Ain't nothing like a bunch of black folk rehashing the wrong somebody don done to them, like a blues song, when wounds hadn't yet healed.

The backstory to his behavior has to be told, so you can see the context of

33

the *family intervention discussion*. On that night, the issue of a fight came up again; my family member got in my uncle's face like they were on the street. She started out fussing and family shouted, "Tell him girl. That don't make no sense."

My family member may still be scarred today from the time she was in seventh grade when she and my uncle got into a physical fight. I mean *a knock down drag out* fight which resulted in my uncle slamming her head to the floor in the presence of my younger cousins and perhaps my daughter who would have been about three or four years old.

When I got to Grandma's from work the day of this fight to pick up my daughter, I was fuming and told Grandma my uncle's behavior was absolutely unacceptable. She made excuses for him and according to family, Grandma told the police he had not fought anyone while all my cousins who witnessed it told the other side of the story to the police. My uncle reportedly told the police, "She don't know what she talking about. She senile. She old and she senile!!" This was many years before we found this to be closer to a truth than we were prepared for. He was a grown man and should have had the decency to know better than to fight with family. My daughter, Joélle loved her uncle though and was most assuredly about the only one as he had a life history of being extremely annoying. It was strange, but I had nothing but contempt for him and he loved her in spite of my differences with him.

My uncle and my family member were about to come to blows all over again on family intervention night. I intervened and told him, "I missed the last fight, but I'm here this time and it ain't go'n be a one sided fight cause you ain't got to beat on a little girl anymore. You got an older opponent now!!!" In hindsight that whole night was absolutely bananas; I was not wearing my master's degree cap at the time. I channeled my inner Roseland just in case he thought he was going to deal out some *arse whoopings*. Grandma sat in the midst of all this chaos seemingly overwhelmed, but also appearing as if she liked all the commotion as she sat with a peculiar, sly grin on her face.

I began to recount to all in attendance one of the stories my older cousin, who we shall call Carmene, told me. Grandma had been seen out at 2 am in the morning at the Chinatown el train station delivering money in the middle of winter to my uncle because he needed to get high. Grandma was in denial of the obvious and did not believe he was a substance abuse despite all the clues he was dropping. Regardless of the number of small appliances that disappeared, or the 25 inch television that mysteriously left Grandma's house, or dresser drawers that were constantly rambled through. She was in utter denial that he did those things or showed herself to be like Mother Theresa, *love them anyway*.

The family got more agitated and began to demand that my uncle change his ways and stop using Grandma in that way causing her possible harm. I believe he added a significant degree of stress to Grandma that her illness didn't need. I gave another account that Grandma had been recently seen walking the streets of Englewood at about 11 pm taking him food and money to an abandoned building on Marquette Road. This was very dangerous and is unconscionable that a son would place his mom at risk like that.

Grandma was retrieved from her bedroom and brought into this conversation questioned by the family asking if she had done such a dangerous thing as she denied it. Grandma got so angry, which was quite rare and quite honestly a bit funny because of the way she showed out. Imagine lil petite, gray haired Grandma standing up, stamping her feet and yelling at the top of her *sweet ole grandma pudding pop sugar-on-top* lungs, with her head thrust back towards the ceiling yelling, "CARMENE IS A LIAR, LIAR, LIAR AND I'LL TELL HER TO HER FACE SHE'S A LIAR. I DID NO SUCH THING!!!!!"

Grandma's Oscar winning rebuttal performance on slander was so tight, she had me thinking that perhaps I was the loon and I misheard what Cousin Carmene had stated and that she fabricated the story. NOT!!! I felt like the family was looking at me like *why are you lying on Grandma like that.* I was worried they thought I was trying to rally support to throw my uncle out of the house with no basis.

Grandma told us to call Carmene and have her tell that story to her face. Well, we did and obliged her demand. Cousin Carmene got out of her bed late at night, drove nine miles to tell the story in almost exact detail of what she originally told me. She had firsthand knowledge about Grandma responding to my uncle's demands that had her out walking the streets and on the bus late at night.

Grandma shook her head from side to side in disagreement and up and down concurring with Cousin Carmene's account. I was confused. Carmene asked Grandma if she remembered that night. That same stamping on the floor hollering Grandma, who had just been fired up minutes before with brimstone and indignation of the allegations and accusations made against her, paused a moment. We paused too like she was *E F Hutton*. You know " *When E F Hutton talks everybody listens!*"

On bated breath we waited for her answer. She said, "Oh yeah, that's right. That's right. That's right. I remember. Sorry." She walked away like we had been discussing the weather. The room paused and we all just looked at one another. In unison, we all fell out laughing; crying to the point of tears marveling at the metamorphic disposition of the malicious slander Grandma felt we were thrusting upon her with her retrieved memory. Dementia does that.

After his death that would occur a short time later, she was stricken with grief, paranoia, feelings of helplessness and heart ache over her son. It is always the one that tugs at your heart the most that can give you much pain. I conceded a little while longer against what I felt was going against my intuition and allowed for my uncle to live there, but he maintained his street life, late night pit stops and petty thievery for a few more months until I insisted we show tough love. It tore Grandma to pieces when I told her he was no longer welcome in the home. He posed a threat to our safety and was caused tension in the home.

My uncle was eventually diagnosed with cancer of the brain, liver and pancreas. Grandma had to let him back home, so he wouldn't die on the streets. After a while, he experienced chronic pain with complications from the opioids to manage his pain. He was bedridden and no one could provide him the care he needed to remain at home. A family decision was made for him to go to a nursing home. Bless her heart, Grandma really tried to do it all and was sick herself. She visited him faithfully just as she had done with *Big Mama*, and others as *Queen of the Sick and Shut In*. She brought him what he asked for, what he didn't need, prayed for him and sat by his bedside like only a mother could with unconditional love.

I felt an enormous amount of guilt because in some way I felt responsible for adding to Grandma's heartache having forced her hand to choose her grand and great grandchildren over her son for our collective safety and some normalcy. She loved him dearly and became more depressed after his move to the nursing home. It was the same facility where her mother died. I was in the midst of my own depression feeling trapped because of the lack of family support to help navigate Grandma's care and my uncle's situation. I couldn't fix this thing that wore on her mind and seemed to progress her illness.

♥ Chapter Reflection ♥

This chapter was not a good example of what to do in a number of ways. I promise we were much more refined and diplomatic in the way we handled Grandma's care. Confrontation never has a good outcome. The expression, **"You can catch more flies with honey than with vinegar"** *should be the standard approach to keep tempers from flaring. If at all possible, try to think up more than 1 or 2 scenarios of issues you face and solve the problem collectively. People will buy into something if they feel they are a part of the decision-making process. Whatever you decide try to go for less impact and be open to other ideas. You can always try it and start again.*

It was complex in that my uncle had a long addiction to drugs and Grandma was an enabler to him all of her life. And just because she was ill, that behavior didn't go away. My role came in conflict as her granddaughter/caregiver/advocate/protector who was delegated by absence of collective decision making to do what was best as I saw fit at that time. Coming together and discussing what was going on was news to a lot of the family while common knowledge for some. My uncle manipulated situations placing Grandma in danger long before I moved in. He took advantage of her love for him. Some survivors' family will be taken advantage of in different ways. It will be hard, but the survivor's care is most important.

Grandma was who she was⁓⁓⁓ as a mother, a wife, an aunt, a sister, a faithful servant, a grandmother, a great grandmother and a genuine friend. It was only natural for her to be the caring woman she was. She stayed on her knees praying and was led by her faith. I am consoled by the fact that she modeled for me in the way we as a people should be. Prayerfully, I endeavor to be a woman of her character. Grandma personified and embodied love, faith, resilience, patience, humility, character and stamina. Hold on to the good and the better days of those you love and allow that to carry you through your own storm. If they can still exist and handle this madness so should you. They need you to be present!

♥ How's the Family?   8 ♥

One of the sisters of the church, the one that had less than wholesome thoughts about my *bad* daughter came by to visit one day while at work. Grandma did not attend church anymore after her series of mini strokes. Visitors were typically embraced, but this visitor was Grandma's *best friend*. My daughter witnessed this one episode and gave me her account of how Grandma's *best friend* carried on.

One of Grandma's signature lines was *"How's the family?"* as she was apt to repeat this phrase a number of times before your visit was over in an effort to make chit chat conversation. Sister Farnes came by our home with another church member while I was at work for a visit with Grandma. Apparently, Grandma opened conversation in her usual manner asking Sister Farnes, *"How's the family?"* She must have asked her multiple times. My daughter, Joélle, went on to say Sister Farnes snapped at Grandma and said, "Sister Passmore, I don't know why you keep asking me how my family is over and over again. How would you like it if I asked you over and over again how's your family? How's your family? How's your family? How's your family?" She was angry and irritated.

I could not believe how one of Grandma's closest friends could be so mean and lack understanding of her disease. Dementia was still unfamiliar to many people at that time, they had little to no understanding of how it manifested itself nor did they recognize what the signs and symptoms looked like.

Regardless of the fact that I made an effort to inform the church about her illness, denial and an unwillingness to accept Grandma's dementia caused people to alienate themselves from her. They didn't know how to deal with the change of her abilities overlooking the obvious. Close family members would do the same rarely visiting or calling her. The Caller ID device actually captured more calls than we thought she was receiving because according to Grandma no one called or came by daily, although Joélle would tell me differently if she was home when the visits occurred.

She looked the same; she smiled the same and granted kisses and hugs to strangers alike all the same. I imagine it was hard not to comprehend *how she could not be the person whom they knew her to be.* Grandma was *the one* who faithfully visited every sick bed of her fellow church members in the home or hospital by bus or automobile, attended all the funerals, baked for many repasts and called to check on a member of the church when they hadn't been seen or heard from. She cared and loved her church with all her heart. She lived and breathed church. It didn't appear that the same love she had shown towards the small congregation was reciprocated.

Later, I would learn that Sister Farnes thought of my young daughter as "bad" because Grandma would put the unexplainable on Joélle. I actually witnessed this myself when Grandma was given charge of the church keys after one Sunday service which I thought was a huge risk on their part to entrust her with the keys to open for the evening service. Grandma's plan was to get something to eat and stay inside the church. I arrived at the church to pick up Joélle and Grandma came out holding the door to give me a mini report and see Joélle off before we drove away.

Grandma stepped away from the door and it shut. She turned to Joélle and said in a quick panic, "Why did you lock that door?" Joélle stood quietly about 4 feet away from the door with shoulders shrugged speechless. I yelled from the car, "Grandma she didn't touch the door! Where are the keys?" She said they were inside. Grandma didn't have a cell phone, so I ended up with a long day going home to review Grandma's contact list and call church members to let them know she was locked out. Grandma waited in a restaurant across the street from the church waiting for someone to arrive and let her in. Grandma would process this experience differently and pin the lockout on Joélle.

♥ Chapter Reflection ♥

Joélle was about 10 years old at that time and unofficially was bestowed the responsibility of being Grandma's caretaker away from home while at church. Her presence with Joélle as her sidekick probably helped Grandma worship where she loved a few more months longer. Her intermittent periods of having it together and falling apart had to have been dismissed by her fellow congregation members as they gave her the keys to the church! It was clear that Grandma needed some companionship to her favorite place in the world and I am thankful Joelle went with her. Sister Farnes' understanding and patience had waned. They traveled down south together and acted as sisters to one another yet her annoyance with Grandma was evident. Dementia does that!

Perseveration, the repetition of repeating phrases over and over again and focusing on a subject can be taxing and annoying. Perhaps if visits were coordinated while someone else was home that might have aided Grandma's company in understanding more about her condition. Maybe if I had a nice card or handout for the visitor as they departed it might have helped them understand what they just went through. Maybe this method of ask might have elicited some support for help and prayer as a caregiver. Maybe we could have had church at home for an hour singing spirituals together. Maybe I could have invited her congregational members over for dinner since she no longer was capable of going to visit them on her own.

Eventually, the repeated questions no longer become a nuisance. You get used to it and you move on. I would have taken that over not hearing her voice any more. I asked my children to respond to Grandma's questions without being argumentative and just answer what she asked offering the rationale that the time exerted to point out to her that she asked you a question already would be less painful if they just responded and moved about with their activities. When it happened again the kids would cut their eyes subtly as if to say she just did it again and my eyes reflected back to them I heard it too, but remember..."

You will have to find forgiveness in your heart a number of times for others and yourself as I hold on to Jesus' directive from Matthew 18: 22 that says something to the effect of Jesus says forgive not seven times, but seventy times seven. It is a struggle, so always start with yourself for not forgiving. I am a work in progress!

It was my daughter Joélle's birthday and we celebrated with a family and friends sleepover. Only this time we were at Grandma's house since this was our new home. Grandma was out doing her usual Saturday errands: beauty shop, cleaners and pay bills. The girls had a great time playing games and did the girlie things that they do. Grandma came home in the midst of all the fun, out of

the rain while I was in the kitchen preparing dinner for the girls. She greeted me in good spirits with a number of bags in hand and her rain scarf. She went in her room to change and time passed. The sleepover party activities went on and except for Grandma, we all retired to bed at about midnight, as it had been a long day.

I was awakened at about 1 am because I heard Grandma rambling again, walking the floor and looking for something. She called up the stairs asking if I saw her sandwiches that she brought in. I told her no and attempted to go back to sleep. The rambling noises continued, so I went downstairs to ask Grandma about the sandwiches. She trembled with tears in her eyes, wore a long-faced puppy dog expression and her voice cracked as she spoke. This was the jist of our exchange:

Her: Taun, somebody stole my sandwiches.

Me: Grandma, who would steal your sandwiches?

*Her: Well, you got company here and those girls probably ate my sandwiches. I came
in here and see them on the table.*

*Me: Grandma those girls didn't take your sandwiches; we got too much food here for
them to want to take it.*

*Her: I put them in the freezer, so I could take them to church tomorrow for lunch
with Sister Farnes, Sister Marks and Sister Cates. I was going to take them out in
the morning to thaw out.*

Me: Well, okay let's look in the garbage.

I checked every garbage can in the house and there was no sign of
sandwiches, wrappers or anything. I scolded her, "Grandma there are no
remnants of these girls having eaten anything. Did they eat the paper too? Did
they eat the paper Grandma?" I know, I know--- this was mean. No excuse, but
I was working on minimal sleep and was extremely exhausted. Grandma
started crying at this point and she was just as frustrated as I was, if not more. I
did not care for digging in the garbage at 2 am.

I stopped feeling sorry for Grandma thirty minutes prior because I was
teetering on irritated, agitated and frustrated all at the same time. She insisted
that she purchased sandwiches and cried like she lost her best friend. By this

47

time, I was convinced that she did not buy any sandwiches. I didn't care how many tears she dropped; there was no evidence to prove the sandwiches existed. I replayed the scenario over and over again in my head going back to when she came in earlier that day. I could not recall her bringing in any food and setting it on the table. Dementia does that.

Morning came and I was sleep deprived, so guess who was *not the happiest camper in the group.* The girls were picked up one by one by their parents. After escorting one child to the door I waved them off good bye, closed the front door and turned around in the foyer. I caught sight of a bag and the scent of food. I'll be damned if I didn't see two plastic bags smelling of guess what—ITALIAN BEEF. Grandma had been up early and stirred about in her room while the girls and I ate breakfast, so I knew she was up. Or perhaps she never went to sleep, I didn't know nor did I care. Can you say irritable?

I grabbed the bag off the coat rack, right next to Grandma's umbrella and stormed towards the back of the house. I do mean stormed with chest heaving, heart palpitating, spitting bullets all the way to the back of the house to the lil sad faced *sugar pop sweet on top pudding pop* Grandma, the heartbroken woman who kept me up all night over some damn sandwiches! Dementia does that. I went right to her bedroom door holding the sandwich bag up and talking crazy like the loon that I was through gritted teeth.

Here are the damned sandwiches you were looking for, right here! They were behind the door all the time! You sat up here and accused these girls of stealing. I told you I

couldn't find the sandwiches and you persisted. You had me feeling bad and second

guessing myself and the girls. And they were right there all the time!

Grandma was irritable and so was I. I showed her the sandwiches in my

funkiest disposition and she responded with a big smile and outstretched arms

for a hug. She spoke in her softest, sweetest lil' ole Grandma *sugar pop sweet on top*

pudding pop voice. She said, "I'm sorry Taun. Please forgive me. I loooove you.

Thannnk you. You know I love you!" I thought to myself *yeah right lady.* The case

of the missing sandwiches had been solved. Grandma took the bags, got

dressed and went to church with her bounty like nothing ever happened.

♥ Chapter Reflection ♥

Grandma created scenarios to fit narratives that made sense to her when she didn't

remember. She told very convincing stories. I stood before her and questioned myself so many

times if I got it wrong. There was considerable frustration because Joélle and I had a number of

sleepless nights for all the late night rambling she did.

Joélle was closest to Grandma of all the great grandchildren as that was her traveling

buddy everywhere. Things changed. Alzheimer's grip got tighter. Joélle got older and she became

Grandma's target of accusations about missing items. Joélle's grades suffered.

She was distracted by the care that Grandma needed. Joélle's attention and focus plummeted. Her grades dropped from Honor Roll, which had been a constant in her grade school years. I made up my mind after several incidents of late night wallet searching under Joélle's mattress that I had to protect and preserve her innocence. The days were numbered as I intended to move before it got worse and save my family.

*It began to feel like persecution, but it was perseveration towards a child by one of the dearest people in her life. I felt guilty and ashamed again for the things I said and the things I thought. I was beginning to not feel like me anymore. I became more depressed. I didn't accept it because I didn't have time to deal with my own needs. Dementia does that. **In the midst of chaos, you can't see the sunshine out the window because the storm clouds hover wherever there is light. Always look for the light. It's there; you have to make an effort to find it.***

Grandma's symptoms were worsening, and I needed help from my family. I utilized my social work skills and somehow convinced my family to convene a family meeting outside of Grandma's house to discuss the next course of action as she was not getting better. I took her to one of her most favorite places to eat—Red Lobster. Since she was a foodie and attended so many birthdays, graduations and life changing celebrations; we went to a place I knew her *long memory* would appreciate. We ordered first and then we assisted Grandma with her meal selection. Grandma had never been short on appetite, so she was quite at home in her favorite place. Dinner came and it felt just like old times again. Grandma commented about some aspect of the food on everyone's plate as it arrived to the table. Her focus then came to my plate which contained crab legs and her attention to them never left. Here was the exchange:

Her: *Ooh, what's that?*

Me: *Crab legs. (Looking at her with the side eye.)*

Her: *I never had crab legs before. (Acting like she was scoping out a pot of gold.)*

Knowing she had them before, she got no argument from me; it would have been pointless. I gave her some more of my crab legs. My son had a portion of the crab legs too. The plate wasn't that big. Two minutes later, Grandma asked again, what was I eating, shaking her head side to side like *Mmmmm mmm good.* Really? She was dead set on getting more of my food with those antics. Her eyes were as big as saucers looking like she had seen a golden turkey on my plate. I broke off another leg with a raised eyebrow and Grandma repeated that she never tasted crab legs before. I looked at my daughter, my daughter looked at me and I looked at my son. I gave my son the signal with my *eye language* that he was not to say anything because I already knew he was going to challenge her.

Earlier on Jonathan had a habit of saying to Grandma, *"Why you keep asking me the same thing over and over again? You asked me how old I was and then you ask me again and again."* I talked with him constantly about making sure to not hurt Grandma's feelings when he would say that to her because *Grandma was sick.* I needed a t-shirt and a baseball cap with big, bold letters **GRANDMA IS SICK!**, so I wouldn't have to say it so much. Perhaps I needed reminding too.

Grandma casually mentioned *again* that she didn't know what crab legs tasted like and I ignored the comment and her. Now she had a plate full of food, but her focus was elsewhere—still in my plate. Dementia does that. My thought was this, *Listen here little old lady who never tasted crab legs three times in all her life in the past twenty minutes. I am not breaking you off another piece of nothing. I am not going another further with this madness.* I called my mother, who broke away from the family meeting, to get an update on their plan to help and share how her Mama was trying to eat up my dinner. Oh, she laughed a hearty laugh. All I wanted to know was when they were wrapping it up, so I could bring that little honey home. Clearly Grandma enjoyed my dinner while my dinner sucked!

♥ Chapter Reflection ♥

I felt like I was on a punked episode with Grandma's love of crab legs that night. The funny found me in this episode because it was a light-hearted episode. I should have bought her own dinner of crab legs to go since she experienced so much joy eating them. It would have been the least I could've done considering what she was going through. That was one of the few times that me and the kids would go out to restaurants with Grandma because she lost the desire to do the things she loved to do the most: eat out and go to church. Her joys faded away just like her memory.

When she later lost the ability to speak and other faculties she was much more amenable to going out, but it would take a lot of preparation. When I got married and moved to the 'burbs, I thought she might enjoy the car ride and the space. She let it be known that she was anxious on these outings and shortly after arriving she would ask, "Is Bobby coming? Does he know how to get here? When is Bobby coming?" She would ask this over and over in any setting when she was away from her home. It is important to know that the familiar surroundings of those surviving Alzheimer's is very important. It offers security and familiarity. This was taken into consideration for our family's decision to keep her home. There were too many haunting stories of maltreatment in nursing care facilities and we decided we would not go that route for her. Granddaddy also helped with that decision because it was not going to happen without his support. Finances were a significant factor for him and he declined supportive living as well.

That family meeting was supposed to create some dialogue about what we could do together to assist Grandma. I cannot recall the outcome and I assure you nothing came of it because I still shouldered the responsibility by myself. They heard what might have sounded like an empty threat for the next few years, "Y'all g'on believe me when that moving truck pulls up and I leave." I finally made good on that promise when I purchased my home in 2005.

Initially, when I did presentations on caregiving and coping with stress I would caution attendees to not do anything like my family as we got it all wrong. Thankfully that narrative changed over time and we eventually got it right. Ok more of us did. Some part of me wants to explore and get behind the story of the individuals around the world who pull back and don't assist in the caregiving. I want to examine their decision making processes, so I can talk to them directly. That would be a great book full of their insight; maybe I should entitle it *What's Scary About Dementia? Confessions of a Non-Caregiver---How I Pulled Back From Doing My Part to Help!*

After one of the local Alzheimer's walks in recent years with friends and family, I stopped a moment to explain to my colleague why my family members developed a separate group that *year while walking separately for the same person. Bananas, right? Well, a woman seated near*

us heard my account of my solo journey at the outset, the lack of participation, the separation

of family and the drama that played out after Grandma's death and she got angry. She said a

few swear words and remarked if they were so damned concern about her care they should have

done their part. She shared that she too had experienced some of the same issues on the

distribution of work and it struck a chord with her and she had a large family. She was of

another ethnicity than mine and it played out like it has so many other times when I talk with

people and they voluntarily share their family experiences. The work usually falls on one or two

and it doesn't matter the race/ethnicity or the amount of money the family has---the problem of

fewer folk helping to carry the load is universal.

♥ Bobby's Daddy Flag   11 ♥

My mother purchased a full-size comforter for my daughter one year that resembled the American flag with the bold red, white and blue coloring and stars. After a few months of use, we began to recognize that the comforter kept disappearing from my daughter's room. Whenever we asked Grandma about it she would deny ever seeing it. We'd look for the blanket only to end up finding it in Grandma's room. We would take it back, wash it and put it back on my daughter's bed. Very soon after its recovery, the comforter would disappear again. This went on like this for about a year.

So we finally confronted Grandma to get an understanding of why she kept taking this particular blanket and asked her why. She replied, "That's Bobby's daddy's flag! That's Bobby's daddy's flag!" She began to yell and got visibly upset, so we'd have no other choice but to back down and let it go. No matter how many times we would explain that it was a blanket, she would still say it was the flag. Arguing was futile.

♥ Chapter Reflection ♥

I can only surmise that the flag meant something to her from her long memory and she recognized its value and wanted to ensure its safekeeping. This particular fixation on a theme that we would live with for a very long time is called perseveration. We should have just given the comforter to her because it caused her distress. We didn't want Alzheimer's to win because it was my daughter's comforter gifted to her by my mom, Joelle's grandmother. My maternal great grandfather, Zire "Jack" Passmore served in World War II and upon his death he was honored with a soldier's funeral which of course includes the presentation of the American flag which had been ultimately given to my grandfather. The real flag was also hidden by my grandmother, as well, so she likely thought we were taking the actual flag from her playing games. Grandma on the surface looked perfectly healthy and showed intermittent signs that she had Alzheimer's. We responded to her as if she was the Grandma we knew because she had more lucid moments than not and seemed "normal" most days. Dementia does that.

I did a presentation at work on Alzheimer's at the request of a colleague. There were some who cried through the presentation, left or came up to me afterwards to share their own battle with dementia. As much as we think of it as something impacting us personally, dementia lives and breathes in our co-workers too and we don't say anything because we probably don't know what to do. Afterwards, it came to my knowledge that a couple of people retired because they had Alzheimer's. Their work was suffering, personality changes were evident and being at work probably made them feel like themselves. It could be your clients, patients, church members, friends or your neighbor. Those knee jerk reactions mean something. Figure out how to do something timely. Tell somebody so that the person suspected of dementia can get the help they need. Science has enabled us to not have to view a corpse's brain in order to get the diagnosis of Alzheimer's or dementia. Be proactive.

57

♥ Bath Time Ordeal 12♥

Like I mentioned earlier, it used to be a big production to get Grandma in the bathtub, but once Grandma accepted baths again, a system was devised and life got better. I wanted to ensure she was fresh especially after she began wearing disposable undergarments. Her cooperation was well received. I respected her privacy and tried to maintain normalcy as much as possible. That was until she began losing her clothing items that were placed inside the bathroom for her convenience. I made random checks and asked her through the door, "Are you alright?" And she would reply, "Yes."

Grandma's stays in the bathroom got longer and longer, so I would knock prior to going in. Then I'd ask her what was taking so long for her to come out. She would tell me she couldn't find her clothes or her *sock*. Her *sock* was her version of a prosthetic filler for her breast that was removed when she had cancer. Double survivor. She put money, ID, and other items in it because the *long memory* of putting things in your bosom meant close keeping. The bathroom was not that large at all. I would look around the toilet, on the back of the bathroom door, in the garbage can, in the tub and be stumped. I found her lost items balled up in the recess area in back of the tub wrapped up in tissue. So I learned to show her the items before she went into the bathroom because she wouldn't get in the tub first, if she didn't see them laid out. She refused to

58

take her bath if I didn't have everything together for her.

If drama didn't occur in the bathroom then it would be the bedroom which was a much bigger space to lose some stuff. Being a pro at finding things became my specialty, when Grandma said she was missing something I immediately went straight to her mattress and lifted it up. Shoes, suits, dresses, night gowns, shoes, boots, books, shoes, snacks and everything else under the sun could be found there. I even found a few of my savings bonds in her mattress that *she put up for me.*

♥ Chapter Reflection ♥

Since the bath time usually ended with a search it was evident she needed more guidance in her bathroom routine. I could have guided her into the tub and made more periodic checks when she got out of the tub during that time when she was on the cusp of not being able to bathe alone. She fretted so much the worry cloaked her. I think we tried using baby monitors to hear motion. There are a myriad of options to select from with visual and auditory supports to help monitor survivors. The value of privacy will compete with safety and their emotional well-being. Decisions need to be well thought out on what to do next and how to do it. Change is hard for the average individual if you consider how impactful change has been to you or those around you. It's worse for the survivor. Imagine what that is like when you feel like you are losing control and are powerless to do anything about it. The survivor needs your help. Navigate it gingerly and let your actions be the least intrusive as much as you reasonably can.

Grandma needed an environment that had a minimalist style in order to decrease the many places she would hide things. She had food, spoons, wet clothing she washed and didn't dry that were mildewed in the most oddest of places. It caused her to cry all the time and lose a lot of sleep because she was always looking for something. Knowing now what I wished I thought of then, I would have taken her chest of drawers out, created a closet system in her closet and used more shelving and baskets or nice crates to organize her items. **Keep it simple.**

She likely needed a weekly cleaning of her bedroom in which the homemakers could have assisted with to keep the buildup of stuff down in her room. Organization and routine is key. The survivors rely on you to keep things in order, so they know what to expect. Consider mealtime, activity time, bedtime, medication time and other moments that require routine. Survivors rely on their long memory and we should not stray away from their systems as much as possible. It can be upsetting. Dementia does that.

♥ The Day Life Changed   13 ♥

Let me set the stage for you if I may, it was winter. I just got off work and came home to start my second shift, caring for Grandma and the kids. Dinner had to be prepped, homework had to be checked, the house needed to be straightened up and there was no time for rest. I literally came home, took off my coat, washed my hands and started preparing dinner without having sat down for at least five minutes.

This chapter too is yet another memorable moment of the intensity of the experiences you encounter in your caregiving. It is locked in my memory like it was yesterday because:

1. *I know the book ain't about me, but I was traumatized and got hurt in the process;*

2. *It was the beginning of the demise of Grandma's ability to be herself; and*

3. *Everything in the world was about to be turned upside down and inside out because*

   Alzheimer's changed the game.

In all of my years as a clinician, I have yet to see something like this play out right before my eyes. Grandma's bedroom was in eyesight right off the kitchen to my left, so I had a clear view to her room. It was noted that Grandma was acting *weird* for lack of a better word, which was very uncharacteristic. You could hear her in her bedroom crying, for what appeared to be no apparent reason stating over and over again that we didn't love her. She got louder and louder. "Y'all don't love me, WAAAAGGGGGHH!"

Each time my daughter or I asked her what was wrong she would simply utter, "Nothing." Grandma was inconsolable, so I continued to navigate dinner prep with a super watchful eye on her while trying to assess the situation and claim my rights to being *Super Social Worker Off Duty Hall of Fame on Second Shift* award dealing with whatever that soap opera episode had to offer.

Grandma's wailing grew louder and louder while at the same time my concern grew too. My daughter, Joélle, going on eleven-years-old at the time watched Grandma with an even closer eye in wonderment of the events that were unfolding minute by minute.

I cannot fully describe Grandma's crazed laughing that ensued after the first bout of crying any better than it sounded like a witch's cackle. She cycled back and forth between the wailing and cackling switching every few seconds. Now Joélle began giggling because I believe she thought Grandma was entertaining her. I scolded Joélle to stop laughing because this scenario was different. Something was wrong and my anxiety was welling in my chest with flutters. My throat felt like it was closing up altering my breathing and creating tension in my body which I imagine felt like a heart attack coming on. I had to remain calm and maintain order in the home without alarming the kids that this thing was spiraling out of control. I was about to explode, but I held it together for the kids. Years later, my chest would suddenly flutter again like that at work for no apparent reason from time to time.

I motioned for Joélle to call Granddaddy and my mom to get to the house quickly. I tried to convince Grandma she needed to go to the hospital, but she refused. Granddaddy got there, but not soon enough for me. My head felt like it was about to explode. In true Granddaddy style he said, "What the hell wrong with you Maggie——why you acting like that?!!" He tried to convince her that she needed to go to the hospital too, but she refused. I called 911 because at that point my heart was pounding in my throat something terrible. The core of my fear was that I lost control and couldn't fix *it*. Dementia does that. Can you imagine living your life and career as a fixer of all things and not be able to fix your own life? Tragic.

I convinced Grandma to come out of her bedroom, she made it about twenty five feet to the living room couch with all this erratic behavior that was so over the top. I was terrified that she had all of a sudden become what looked to be insane. That's how bad it was. After several more lonnnng minutes of coaxing, I got Grandma near the front door and without warning she dropped it like it was hot and landed with dead weight right across my feet. I screamed in pain because she really hurt my leg and we were stuck in the foyer measuring about three feet wide or less struggling with the storm door and wind whipping through the house, but she wouldn't move.

Now mind you, Grandma was a petite, stout woman, at that time, standing 4'11" weighing in at 215 pounds on her little round frame. She fell out on the floor screaming, that she didn't need to go to the doctor. Grandma yelled more loudly, "Police! Police, somebody help me!" in her still *sweet ole pudding pop with sugar on top* Grandma voice as I attempted to get her off the floor. She was dressed in a full slip and an open button-down granny gown and pantyhose on an extremely bitter, cold Chicago night in February. I seriously, seriously strained an already tender back that survived three car accidents and pulled a muscle in my back trying to get her off the floor causing an unbelievable pain that lasted for weeks.

In both our infinite wisdom, my then seventy-three-year-old Granddaddy and I decided that we would pick up 215 pounds of dead weight, take her down the steps, across the yard, out the gate and put her in the car. Needless to say, that was not a good idea and it didn't work out the way we planned at all. *What had happened was* she ended up being half in the house half out the house lying on the porch dressed in her standard issue Grandma uniform. One had the legs and the other the arms and we somehow got her up. It was about 20 degrees Fahrenheit; she fought us both from trying to get her to the hospital and suddenly she dropped dead weight again to the porch floor gripping the wall like someone was trying to kill her.

Trust--- my thoughts were all over the place and I promise it wasn't *nothing nice.* She put me through a thing because she wore my A double S out, so I'm gonna plead the fifth on that one. When I tried to get her back in the house she responded with more screams again shouting "Police, Police, Police!" over and over again in that same *pudding pop with sugar on top* voice in the sweetest way possible. She had such a fierce grip on the door.

All I could think of outside of the fact that she could possibly cause harm to herself is: *What the hell is taking the paramedics so long to get here? Where is my mother? and lastly Lord, people are go'n think I am over here really beating on this woman!*

I struggled to get Grandma inside and she fell on my leg again which sent extremely sharp pain bolting through my already stiff arthritic knee and the strained muscle in my back. Childbirth contractions could not compete with the pain of that day. I was winded, crying with my hair all over my head looking possessed. My son, 3 1/2 years old at the time, grabbed one of Grandma's legs trying to assist me. I seemed to be in more distress than his Great Grandma. Oh boy were we a sight to see. It was definitely one of those *had to be there moments* to get the fullness of how chaotic that episode played out.

In the midst of all this physical activity, that woman became possessed like the Bionic Woman. I called one of the kids to bring me a coat or blanket to put on top of her while I waited for somebody, anybody to show. The paramedics finally pulled up in front of the house and that woman, my sweet dear, then seventy-one-year-old Grandma, literally jumped up off the porch floor the moment the fire truck pulled up, like a sixteen-year-old high school cheerleader. Grandma said, *"Why are y'all here? What's going on? What's happening? Y'all didn't come here for little ole me, did you?"* I thought to myself, *I'll be God $#$%@!!@.*

You had to see that *sugar honey iced tea* to believe it with your own eyes. I looked at her in disbelief, ankle throbbing, knee burning and back was about to bust open from the muscle spasms of that night's antics like we did not have a 45 minute ordeal. Grandma smiled, walked back in the house so nicely and ladylike allowing the paramedics to do what they do. I stood in the doorway, stunned—looking at her metamorphosis back to normal. She declined the ambulance ride and agreed to accompany me in my car. Needless to say my heart rate was pretty elevated. Hell, I needed my own vitals to be checked.

They left. She waved bye to the *"nice people."* The kids and Grandma beat me to the damn car. I was a mess—physically, mentally and emotionally all over the place. I jumped in the car rushing to the local hospital feeling like I was on two wheels and literally almost hit somebody going through the ER driveway. I had so much adrenaline in me, I couldn't see straight. Grandma got out of the car willfully and walked into the hospital as if nothing ever happened.

Unbeknownst to us life would never be the same for any of us after that night. Grandma was hospitalized for one and a half weeks as her blood sugar had to be brought under control. It was at 600. We later found out she suffered six mini strokes otherwise known as TIA, transient ischemic attack, a temporary blockage of blood flow to the brain. That in combination with her

66

dangerously high glucose levels and Alzheimer's, doctors stated that, it was surprising that she had not gone into a diabetic coma. They stabilized her sugar levels. When she was discharged, she was a completely different woman than she went in leaving a shell of body with little signs of joy in her life. She would never attend church again. She lost her desire to clean house, cook, bathe, leave the house, go to the doctor and to eventually speak.

♥ Chapter Reflection ♥

*After one year and three months, Grandma suffered those mini strokes and none of us was prepared for the change in her character and personality. Every now and then Grandma would swear in a slick kind of way a short time after that and we would be asking, "Did she just cuss?" Her temperament changed. She was argumentative, and stayed up all night looking for keys, clothes, bibles, stockings, glasses and the list goes on and on. It was rough and then things calmed down. The change in Grandma created a wave of change in our family system and it has never been the same since her diagnosis and worsened even after death. I am confident if I had not been betrothed **the sole responsibility** of being her caretaker, if others were there to help her and communicated what they experienced we could have been proactive. We would've put our gear on for battle. Instead we all eventually licked our wounds and put on our ill fitted armory to tussle with Alzheimer's again and again. We did get smarter though once we embraced that it was not a job you could do alone **and** do well. It is complex enough.*

♥ Comcast 523   14♥

Grandma loved western television shows. She used to watch the programs and start thrusting and thrashing during the fight scenes as if she was in the scene herself. She got lost in the many programs that she remembered like *Gunsmoke, The Rifleman, Bonanza, Maverick, The Lone Ranger* and those good ole movies like *High Noon, Arrowhead* and *Gunfight at the O. K. Corral.* Those were classic programs that both Grandma and Granddaddy loved. The kids and I came over and wanted to switch over to a channel we wanted to watch and would get cussed out for changing the channel. "Hey, Maggie is watching the God d*mned television station. What's wrong with you? Turn it back to 523!"

The channel stayed on 523 when Grandma was seated and positioned in her spot on her Lazy Boy chair where you could find her nodding her head to the side doing a little jig in her seat looking as if she was humming to herself. She was comfortable, freshly bathed, hair combed, all lotioned up and would have eaten dinner already. She watched show after show. That was the time to catch up on paperwork, bills or tending to personal care like clipping fingernails and toenails or a foot massage. It was then we could change the channel to catch our programs. In minutes, she would be asleep with her head cocked to the side and mouth open getting a good nap in. Now Granddaddy on the other hand loved CNN, BBC and CLTV. He threw a little FOX network in there too, so he could

68

really get a lot off his chest about what them "rotten motherf*rs was trying to do" and "Ain't that right Maggie" She would be his amen corner and co-sign what he said with a dry as toast response with a hint of *Imma act like I care* on it, "Yeah Bobby!"

Granddaddy's programs trumped everybody's television preferences because you was go'n learn something that day as long as he was there. He was so into politics and one of the entry questions if you came into the house was *"Do you watch the BBC?* Motherf*rs around here don't know nothing! You got to see what the people on the other side of the world is talking about." Come in there and say you don't watch one of those three channels and he was go'n talk about you behind your back, *like a dog* as they used to say.

Granddaddy was very opinionated and from the time when Grandma was speaking 'til she couldn't speak anymore--- he never stopped asking Grandma questions and trying to engage her in conversation. *"Whatcha think about that? You hear what the motherf*r said or don' did?"* He was exhibiting normalcy. Even when he knew he wasn't going to get a response he attempted to keep her engaged regardless of the hold *Mr. Alzheimer's* had on her voice.

He would comb his hair and then he'd roll his office chair beside her and comb her hair sometimes with an ever so gentle touch. That was his intimacy and his way of connecting with her. Every now and then he would start reminiscing about Grandma's *big pretty legs*, how she used to dress and the length

69

of her hair. I never been to Ellis Park, but I show nuff feel like I been there. That was where they met when they were just young adults. In those moments, I just lied down on the couch in the dining room and just listened. All I had to say was "yep, unh hmm and naw" to let him know I was listening as he gave whoever was listening a peace of his mind.

Perhaps he was acting as Grandma's memory for her when he went down that road of recollection as he often did. Maybe he thought it was meaningful for her to know he remembered when they first met and what attracted him to her.

Now these speculative thoughts are in hindsight of them not being present on earth anymore, but it makes me wonder. What was the intent of his conversations? Who was he talking for? Was it for her, his wife and companion who couldn't remember any of her grandchildren's names? Was it for me, the self-proclaimed family historian? Or was it to remind himself of what life was like when things were better?

Granddaddy had no filter and several of my friends and other family members would come over and one of the first things he would say is "Me and your Grandmama ain't had sex since 1967!" Why he felt the need to make this random public service announcement, I do not know, but he did. It undoubtedly made everybody he told crack up laughing. Grandma never batted an eyelash. She never responded or queried him about why he was "telling their business."

They were who they were and it was their narrative. Soon the conversation would turn to politics; he was hard on everybody; even our 44th President was not exempt from Granddaddy's wrath. Let's just say the words, black, Motherf*r and the n word were used interchangeably with lots of vigor on some topics. Earlier on he would ask me, "You think I should take your Grandmama to vote?" I would tell him that would be nice, but it probably wouldn't be a good idea considering she wasn't aware of who she was voting for and why. It had been a part of their routine together something they always did together.

They were perfect for each other even though they were the extreme opposites. I thought him to be amusing while others considered him mean. His delivery was not the best, but he was true to his character and spoke TRUTH every chance he got! You had to at least "put some respect" on his truth because he demanded it.

♥ Chapter Reflections ♥

The routines of the survivor and spouse or partner or very much a part of the fabric of their lives and should be respected. You know how you remark to yourself I wish I would have asked this or I wished I would have asked that after a person is sick or gone? I did ask questions and wish I would have asked some questions with more depth and that I would have written all his funny colloquialisms down.

I have an open heart for a really good western movie and when I watch them I can't help but think of them. Just as much as I can't help but think of what Granddaddy would be hollering about now with the current individual in the White House after President Obama. He would have plenty of source material for months on end weighing in on all that is going on in the world if he were alive. Politics are inseparable from my thoughts of Granddaddy just as western movies are inseparable from my memories of grandma.

Go to those places of comfort when you miss them. Draw on how you felt in those happy moments with the survivor and his or her spouse/partner.

♥ *I Love You* 15 ♥

God grant me the SERENITY to accept the things I cannot change:

COURAGE to change the things I can and

WISDOM to know the difference.

Reinhold Niebuhr

If you are religious, spiritual or just need a visual reminder of an encouraging word you should post the first verse of the Serenity Prayer written by Reinhold Niebuhr in plain sight.

As a caregiver, you quickly learn how to navigate life differently because time is limited and becomes too precious to be mired in bitterness. Lamenting over things you have no control over is futile. Organization and schedules are everything. You can become overwhelmed and feel compelled to walk away from time to time.

Completely walking away was not an option for me. I could not walk away from the woman I loved because she helped mold me into the *rough around the* *edges* version of her. Grandma was soft, quiet, patient, endearing, committed, faithful and loyal to everyone she knew. She set the foundation for what Christian living looked like devoting herself to God and putting God first in everything she did.

73

When I was a live-in caregiver, I grew to be a two-hundred-and-forty pound uncomfortable, sleep deprived, fatigued woman. Everything was heavy. Depression and feelings of hopelessness settled in nicely and cloaked me for a long time. *I knew if I didn't change my situation, the situation was going to change me permanently----perhaps to an earlier death or severe health complications.* But doing respite was different because it had been on my terms: Sunday afternoons. I did what I could and all I couldn't do somebody else had to do the rest.

I had a few *come to Jesus moments* with myself and a few folks when I was relegated to primary caregiver even **after** I moved out. The work always whittles down unfairly to one or two individuals. Close family members refused to engage in Grandma's care which was extremely frustrating. Most people I talk to share the same experiences regardless of the size of their families or support systems.

I had a full-time career, volunteer duties, young children, a new home to manage and I commuted back to Grandma's house to pick up prescriptions, fill pill boxes, bathe and comb her hair every weekend. It wasn't right, and it just wasn't the way she lived her life for someone to behave in that manner and not help. You have to get past your frustration and resentment, or you will be bitter.

Nothing like a bitter caregiver taking care of someone; it doesn't usually go over well with the survivor! I could have become more bitter about the help Grandma *wasn't receiving*, walked away or be the person she helped raised me to be caring from the heart. I felt it was my duty and obligation to care for her as she was my elder and I owed Grandma that much for all she did for me.

The stress of it all helping from outside the home was a whole 'notha story in itself. One thing I know for sure is that you cannot control other folk's behavior. Accept this truth. You can't. If you try, you might have thoughts about hurting somebody and it isn't helpful to your spirit at all. My mom went through it during her turn as caregiver too and she couldn't shake it from her spirit. I tried to counsel her through her anger, but she couldn't wrap her mind around why family would fall back and not assist in helping. In my opinion, they contributed to the decline of my mother's chronic health condition to this day. No one person should have to bear this alone regardless of how big the contribution is—some help is better than none.

There were times that we would visit and it would be evident that no one did basic things regularly. I found myself having to do various tasks beyond coming to help because if I didn't, it wouldn't get done. Period. Family members who were supposed to be the live-in caregivers at the time technically resided with her, but they stayed out of the home all day only to return after 10 pm. It was like she was living alone which negated the mandate from the doctor that she required 24-hour supervision. I used to be saddened and angry by this, but eventually I released what others did and my family got it together with a more planful, coordinated way of caring for Grandma and assisting Granddaddy.

It all started with doing what me, my sister, my daughter, my son and my mom needed to do while establishing a plan for how we intended to do it. My son, Jonathan even as a preteen and adolescent had his part, sweeping the floor, taking out the garbage, answering the phone, watching Grandma if I had to run to the corner store and most of all keeping Granddaddy occupied with conversation when he was around. Sunday afternoons in the car have been forever changed. There is something amazing that happens when I am in my car on Sunday between hours of 1:00 and 2:30 pm, it takes me back to our respite days. Jon and I would make the trek from the south suburbs to the city and it was a ritual that brings with it warm and fuzzy feelings that do not bring sadness, but a smile. I enjoyed my Sunday drive and embraced them without ever feeling burdened. Maybe it is my grandparents' spirit covering us with their presence because that is just how much love we had for one another, unconditionally.

This was comparatively different than the weight and responsibility of being a thirty-something-year old, with two small children, an extremely stressful position as a child abuse investigator, demands of me as an active member of my church, Trinity United Church of Christ Counseling Ministry and the local Chicago Chapter of the National Association of Black Social Workers was a bit much back then.

Joélle assisted with hair and bath time too. We didn't want the bulk of the responsibility, but it was what it was. We called a family meeting a couple of times and no one else showed up. It was just us, my mom and her lineage. Other folks finally fell in line with the program, but it didn't happen overnight. We were thankful when help came because it was too much to carry on our own.

My mom, daughter, sister and aunt all had different approaches to bath time that was seemingly a very important aspect of her life. I don't know why we were so dead set on Grandma having to take a bath rather than wash her up, but we did. One of my routines, when I arrived, was developed out of necessity for bath time to keep the rhythm of the day going. There was often no indication of when was the last time she was bathed because of the lack of communication from those who were supposed to be doing it. I enjoyed getting the bath time routine together, but I had to put everything in the bathroom first.

Grandma had always been a bubble bath fanatic with every kind of Avon colored bottle you can think of adorning her bureau since I was a little girl. I ran the water extremely hot because by the time we finally made it to the tub the water was perfect for her. While the water was being drawn, I would usually have her use the restroom while I multi-tasked and took her hair down. Then I would finish that and gather her slip, undies, bath towels, housecoat, socks and lotion. I had a cold pitcher of water available to temper the water in the event Grandma made up her mind to get in the tub sooner than later.

I gave her time to bathe because the *long memory* was still there to go through the motions. That gave me time to start dinner. I watched her and prompted her from the doorway while perched high on a stool or an ottoman with either my cell phone, a magazine or in eyesight of the TV. Sitting outside of the bathroom threshold was to give some semblance of privacy although the door was open. "Wash this grandma, now wash that. Did you get ...? Did you wash it good?" were a few of the statements I'd make to keep her engaged in the process for as long as she could.

I came in and assisted her explaining what I was doing step by step, talking, singing, humming and talking to let her know I knew she still existed on the inside. I would ask her if she needed me to wash her back and she would respond yes and thank you. Sometimes she would say, "Oh that feels good Taun. Thank you."

Washing her hair could be a trick in and of itself coupled with how to do it gracefully without getting soap in her eyes. I would take a wet washcloth, wet her hair with it, apply shampoo, conditioner sometimes and then use the wet wash cloth over and over again to get it all out. At one point, I had a special cup with a rubber edge & a handle. You would fill it with water and pour on her hair without it getting in her face. I took great care to make her comfortable. She would then get out and I would help dry her off, lotion her up, put her in her night clothes, oil her scalp, style her hair; clip her fingernails and toenails and massage her feet. Imagine getting this pampered experience all the time.

One particular day resonates with me as my all-time favorite moment with Grandma. I call it the day I will never forget. She was super cooperative and gave me no resistance or excuses whatsoever to not get in the tub. I thanked God for that as bath time was a bit of a battle some days. Grandma turned to me while in the tub, looked me in my eyes and said, "I loooooooove you. You are so good to me." She reached for my face, pulled me close and kissed my cheek. Love did that. Priceless. I fought back tears and told her I loved her too. That that was one of those lucid moments when Grandma's spirit pushed through the Alzheimer's to let me know she appreciated my expression of love for her. It was the essence of her that shone through. It reminded me of my purpose in her life.

I think about that day and I feel her love. Sometimes I well up, wish I could hold her again and love on her like only a grandchild can do. Moments like that made me feel like everything was right with the world regardless of what she endured, she was going to be alright. I know Grandma made her mark into heaven's glory for the loving, devoted God-fearing woman she was.

I got mad with God that day and questioned Him. *Why would this woman who lived her life all for His glory suffer through an unforgiving disease like this? When was the cure coming, so people like Grandma could be healed from this condition?* Years later, I would have a chance meeting with Pastor Jason Perry whose mom also lived with Alzheimer's; he helped support his sister in the caregiving of their mother. His sister, Ardella Perry-Osler, wrote a book as well entitled, *Learning to Love Olivia; A Daughter's Journal of her Mother's Journey Through Alzheimer's*. Reverend Perry said to me, "Rain falls on the just and the unjust." My ex-husband, Dwayne, told me "Sh*t happens and sometimes it happens to you." While others would ask, "Why? Why not?"

I wanted the Grandma I grew up with back, the one who could pray away all your fears and worries. I wanted the Grandma who could settle your heart and your mind with an encouraging word. I wanted her to stop slipping into those periods of solemn quietness where one would wonder what she was thinking or what does she want to tell me that she can't.

Grandma lived beyond the ten-year average life expectancy the experts cited during that time. It depends on the type of dementia, age of the person and health. Grandma got so much more healthier with good consistent care that eventually she was no longer diabetic and wasn't insulin dependent anymore. Her appetite remained the same as when she was two-hundred-pound Grandma even though she was a ninety-pound grandma.

♥ Chapter Reflection ♥

Every minute I spent with my grandmother regardless of how hard or painful, my memory of it diminishes with that awesome affirmation of her love for me that day she randomly told me she loved me. It was as clear as anything she ever said in life. You have to really look for those moments when they are lucid and they push pass the Alzheimer's to let you know they are still who they are on the inside like a butterfly nesting in its cocoon transforming.

I haven't met a family yet that didn't have tumultuous experiences, but there is always a chance of making things better. Never let go of your hope that this too shall pass. Your faith is drawn from the sustenance of hope. You push until you can't push anymore for people to step up. If you can't get help from within then be mindful it is okay for you to ask extended family, other friends, church members, sorority/fraternity members to help as well. You have to be intentional to build a village if you don't have one. Pride has no room in this part of your life.

Overwhelmingly, caregiving comes from mostly women. Men typically have a much harder time providing care in general, but most especially the personal care part of it is uncomfortable for them when the survivor is female. **Even if you have a big family, somehow the responsibility is typically unbalanced. Be prepared for that.** *Everyone should assist with whatever skill sets they have to do their part.*

The role of children cannot be dismissed in helping add to the quality of life when families work in partnership with one another. Not only did my son help, but I also engaged much younger family members in playing balloon volleyball with Grandma, painting her nails, brushing her hair, reading to her or dancing. There is something about kids and pets that just change the aura of the room when around older people regardless of their abilities.

Rather than laboring on what the survivor can't do, relish in all that they can and embrace it. *Don't focus on the memory because for right now you can't get it back. Preserve the dignity of the person as much as you can and* **help them to remain independent for as long as they can with the things that are still within their ability to do.** *Lastly, when you rest everything on love like Jesus said, nothing else matters as love eventually conquers all.*

81

♥ *Here he is! Here he is!*   *16* ♥

When I picked up the few chapters of the book to begin my revisions, I had not seen them in over five years. I read this one first; I cried and laughed so hard I woke up my son because I was hysterical with laughter. It was so funny I called my mom and woke her up at one o'clock in the morning to read the story to her and I couldn't finish it properly because I was crying and squealing so much. There is a bit of swearing in it to keep the true essence and spirit of who my Granddaddy was in this story. I hope you enjoy it as much as I do.

My Granddaddy was truly an old school dude. No joke, he was a cross between Fred Sanford from *Sanford & Son* and Archie Bunker from *All in the Family* all perfectly bundled up in one. He was most definitely a ***tell it like it is shoot straight from the hip survival of the fittest if it ain't rough it ain't me***

 kinda man with a rarely seen soft side. Granddaddy worked, lived and breathed construction work practically all of his life, but oh did he love children. He loved, loved, loved pets even more. He engaged so much better with animals than people it was unbelievable. He once told me, "If it wasn't for this motherf*n cat I woulda left your Grandmama a long time ago!" Really

Granddaddy, the cat kept you around? As crazy as it sounded he made you believe he meant what he said.

Now this tough as steel man who cemented the heating vents of the house to the wall when the screws fell out doted over cats. This is the same man who would take the toilet up from the floor, use his bare hands to clear the pipe and tell you what stopped it up, who did it and when. Granddaddy had simple pleasures in life. He had cats named Blackie, Sandy, Brownie and Smokey. Do you see a pattern here? He loved having snacks around for the kids and always encouraged them to play with the cats. Few people saw the lighter side of him because one had to focus on his actions and not so much on what he said.

Well, Granddaddy was gifted with a new kitten that he didn't want because he thought it was way too young. Granddaddy actually loved cats; he just didn't like them too small. He felt the same way about babies. He was both surprised and annoyed by the gift of a six-week old kitten affectionately named, "The Little Motherf*r" because he said it was "just tooooo damned little." I'll call him TLM for short. "No sensible person would take a little motherf*n cat like that away from its mama. It ain't even finished weaning." I had to endure the ranting and the raving about for a good minute and then he would move on.

He already had a really, really **OLD** cat named Cleveland who I dubbed Rasta *Cat aka Clevie* because his hair was so thick and matted in spots that the toilet brush could not reach. Yes, I said toilet brush, but it was solely dedicated for brushing Clevie. It only got at the surface hairs though. Poor thing! Granddaddy called him his *Lucky Cat.*

One time my family visited, the kids talked with Granddaddy. I talked to Grandma and my *then husband* was reading the paper. Clevie walked out from the back of the house to the front where we all were. Just as he entered the living room in mid stride Rasta Cat fell on the floor to the side like a brick with a thud. I recall my then husband peering from around the paper like *what the hell was that* and simultaneously the banter and talking stopped. We all looked in amazement trying to see if he was alive or what. We locked eyes with one another and just guffawed and laughed 'til our stomach hurt. We still chuckle about that to this day.

Granddaddy was like, "He do that some time." Rasta Cat got up and kept it moving like nothing happened. Granddaddy was adamant that he was not going to let the Vet put him to sleep. He said he would let him die nobly at home and he had an excuse every time I would question him about even getting Rasta Cat a haircut. He would yell, *"It's go'n cost me a hundred dollars to get his hair cut."* He would go on to say he didn't know how much longer his *Lucky Cat* was going to live; I guess it furthered his point of why he wouldn't make the investment.

Granddaddy called me to come see his new cat, TLM aka TJ. Clevie aka Rasta Cat had been recovering from a stroke a few weeks prior to my visit. He was on medication, under the care of a doctor and he already had been diagnosed with arthritis. Every time he took a step, I just envisioned Rasta Cat saying "oooh, aaah, ooooh aaaah aaaaah." It looked like with each step he took, it was doing a job on his hips. Do they have hips? I don't know, but Clevie walked with a limp, just like Granddaddy when his gout flared up.

Admittedly, I was excited to finally get to see the *baby cat* since I heard so much about him. I stopped by on my way home after work to see TLM. Grandma greeted me at the door with open arms and a hug as she usually did. I said to her, "I heard y'all got a new visitor. I come to see him." It was clear as Grandma walked away that she didn't have a clue who I was talking about. I came on in and went to the dining room in the dark, I saw that Granddaddy was busy looking for something with a perplexed look on his face. He was moving stuff around walking from the dining room to the spare room he used for storage; clearly he was looking for TLM.

So while he continued his search I decided to sit down reading through a couple of old newspapers out of his stack and some mail. About five minutes later, Grandma said, "Guess who I got?" I looked up in great anticipation only to see her holding up Rasta Cat. I said, *"No Grandma, y'all got a new baby cat. Granddaddy is looking for the baby cat."* Just then Granddaddy hollered from the spare room, "Maggie!! Maggieeeeee, do you see the cat?" She replied, "He was just right here." So she started moving some chairs around and looked under the dining room table and I couldn't figure out for the life of me why they didn't

85

turn the lights on to look for TLM, but okay. A few minutes later Grandma spoke in her super sweet sugar pop pudding on top grandma voice saying, *"Here he is! Here he is!"* And again it was Rasta Cat. Now I was hip to the fact, clearly, she didn't have any knowledge of the TLM kitten being there, so *I was not* going to be moved again by her findings.

Yeeeeeeessss, I did eventually get up to try and help find the kitten myself to no avail. I sat down in the dining room with Granddaddy who was still engrossed in finding that kitten and conversed with him for a minute. Grandma was right there listening and nodding to the conversation. I was all in listening to Granddaddy then I heard Grandma say, *"Looka here. Look at that there!"* smiling like she won the lottery. "Guess who came to see you? "Here he is, here he is!" she says. And with the same super sweet, sugar pop pudding on top with grandma voice, but way more sing songy this time, she pointed at *Rasta Cat* who came from under the dining room table. It was at that point, I guess Granddaddy reached his limit. He burst out raw and in charge with a roar and yelled, *"GOD DAMN IT MAGGIE, I'M LOOKING FOR THE MOTHERF*N KITTEN. THE BABY CAT. I'M NOT LOOKING FOR THAT BIG MOTHERF*N CAT. I AM LOOKING FOR THE KITTEN. DON'T-PICK-THAT-OLE-ASS-CAT-UP-NO-GOD DAMN MO'!*

And with that, it was time to go, exit stage left, go home and try again another day. I chuckled all the way home, but I also felt his frustration beyond his words and felt the pain of his life because it was just too damn hard to understand.

♥ Chapter Reflection ♥

I really wished I could have made the situation right and helped him understand that this was the course of the disease. I wished there was a way I could have given him more of a break than my Sundays. I wish I could have hugged them both and told them it was go'n get better, but I couldn't. In the words of Granddaddy, "Your Grandma just gettin' worsa." To which my response would be, "I know Granddaddy, I know."

Of course, Granddaddy probably didn't see the humor in that episode I described, but for me I had to hold on to the humor because it was my primary mode of coping with the stress. I ended up getting TLM shortly after that for a few months and gave him back to Granddaddy. By that time, TLM was acting feral, but Granddaddy had unconditional love for him in spite of all the scratches and manic running through the house. Rasta Cat and TLM kept him company to deal with the loneliness of not having a verbal exchange with Grandma because she was slowly going into the stage where she stopped talking.

Even with Grandma's illness, TLM never scratched her and often sat by the side of her lazy boy chair as if he was security while scratching Granddaddy up on his arms and ankles. Pets seem to have a sense about those who are ill. Pet therapy does provide a cathartic experience for people especially older individuals. They also offer companionship addressing isolation, relieving boredom and reducing agitation.[6]

Most caregivers' health begins to deteriorate when caring for someone with Alzheimer's or other related dementia because the weight of it all is too much to bear without adequate support. I cannot stress enough that regular medical appointments are necessary to address things earlier on. You don't have to choose your health over the survivor's; it is possible to do both. Take care of them and you.

[6]Cherniack, E. P., & Cherniack, A. R. (2014). The Benefit of Pets and Animal-Assisted Therapy to the Health of Older Individuals. *Current Gerontology and Geriatrics Research, 2014*, 623203. http://doi.org/10.1155/2014/623203

Denial 17 ♥

Granddaddy's take on Grandma's illness in the beginning and middle was that he characterized her as *acting stupid* or *putting on*. He didn't get that Grandma was sick as I explained repeatedly to him over the years. He was old school and it was beyond his understanding that her brain didn't function like it used to anymore. My mom would sometimes get caught up at times too thinking that some of Grandma's actions were intentional at times. He didn't understand why she stayed up all night. He didn't comprehend that she couldn't remember what she had eaten.

Of course, what frustrated him most was that she moved things, especially his things. My keys were taken once when I set them down on the table and they disappeared. All it took was that one time and I made a habit of putting them inside my coat pocket, in a bag outside of view or out of sight. A family member was in town once to evangelize at a church and Grandma swiped her bible with all her sermon notes in it; she spent a couple of hours trying to locate it to no avail. She vowed that she was going to put off visits with Grandma for a while. Things that looked familiar to Grandma would fall into *the black hole*. Her bedroom was a gold mine because the dresser, closet, inside the box spring and inside the pillow all became places where she liked to store things.

There were very few times that I would leave the house when I was living with Grandma because it was too difficult to negotiate for someone to watch her. I had some event just over the Illinois border in Indiana, no more than forty five minutes away from the house. Granddaddy accepted the duty to watch Grandma for the weekend. We returned home to find that individuals who solicit door to door had come by the house selling home alarm systems. He signed a three-year contract and had the alarm system installed. It was against my wishes and we argued a good while about what sense it would make to install an alarm for someone who had an issue with memory having lost too many sets of keys to count, could not recall her pin number to her debit card and was beginning to show signs that her memory was fading. In his mind, he felt that it was the best thing to do for Grandma to help keep her safe. From the man's man point of view perhaps he thought that it would alert us to her comings and goings if she began to wander. He was worried about her wandering which only happened a handful of times.

There were times when I went over for my respite days and he would attempt to start up a conversation with Grandma asking this same line of questions and comments: *Do you know who that is? That's Shi Tahn! Maggie you don't know who that is. That's your granddaughter. That's Barbara Jean's daughter.* Then he would shake his head and mumble it was shame. Then a visitor would come and the cycle would start again with the company. He did that for a long time and he didn't understand how defeating that was to her when she was present in the moment and understood what he said.

The small living room was the center and hub of activities at Grandma's and Granddaddy's house because that was where the television was placed. It was also the room where visitors would usually plant themselves. Granddaddy's desk was in the corner of the living room where he would eat, sit, take his medication, read the paper, conduct business and most importantly watch his politics and sports. All day long he flipped channels and discussed politics because he had a lot to say about it. Granddaddy asked Grandma questions about topics discussed on the news and waited for her to offer her opinion. He waited for her to respond. I guess he was holding on to hope.

Very early on I would come over and upon arrival I would ask Granddaddy what Grandma ate that day. *"Hell, I don t know. I told her a@## to go'n back there and get something to eat. I've been sitting her watching the God damn news."* There were many arguments we had relating to his denial of Grandma's capacity over the years. He just didn't get it.

♥ Chapter Reflection ♥

*One of the things that some **people don't anticipate in caregiving is the working relationship and buy-in required of the spouse or partner.** Spouses/Partners do not always take kindly to people coming in their home, setting up camp and telling them what they will do. Place this in context of your own relationships and imagine* the situation happening to you, if perhaps you broke a leg. Imagine your mom shows up at your door with a suitcase with the intent of staying with you until you are back on your feet which has been estimated to be about six months. She tells your spouse/partner of her plans and proceeds to go to her room and act as if she is a part of the household. I don't surmise that it would go over well or exactly like that. We lose our manners and forget the social norms of asking permission or requesting a family discussion of what their thoughts are on the matter. They can see it as intrusive or more like "taking over" their house.

Granddaddy was fixated on the abilities of Grandma that would show up intermittently and it confused him. He did not understand how she could have a good day or a good moment and then in the next she would be shrouded in confusion or regress to something else.

The best thing I can offer for you to consider and do is to have a one to one with the spouse/partner and discuss your concerns. Have some dialogue about the facts of what is actually going on and what are the possible remedies to right the situation with a listening ear. Only use "I" statements versus "You need to do..." or You are not doing...", so it doesn't come off as blaming or being . For example, I think Grandma might need a little more help now with cooking and cleaning since she has been struggling with her chores lately. Shape it so the spouse, partner or decision maker sees what is in it for them. How does your being there help them? Bottom line.

Granddaddy moved back home as Grandma's symptoms were worsening. One particular day Granddaddy went out to run some errands and hang out. Upon his return home, the house was empty. No Maggie. His first words to me were "Somebody don came in here and stole Maggie." I know I said something smart like "Granddaddy nobody steals black people." This incident kicked up our awareness several notches in terms of the real and true dangers that threatened her safety as this was a new development.

It all started with a cinnamon roll. Granddaddy had an affinity for sweets

and yes he was diabetic too. This was fuel for the small fire Grandma set when she attempted to microwave it. She didn't know how to work the microwave, as it was, and she caused the house to fill with smoke. And the story unfolds.

Granddaddy was still adjusting to the new rules and decided to run some errands at about 6 pm and he didn't return until about four hours later. Thus, the high level of anxiety in his call to me as though Grandma was in one of the sequels of *Taken*. I was awakened to a frantic call by Granddaddy who was emphatic that "Somebody don stole Maggie!" Now what kind of mess is that for an opening line late at night? I had to process what he was saying waking up from my slumber and assured him that nobody took Grandma. I would later find out that she really had been *taken*. I was always Granddaddy's first go to for everything, but I didn't live in the city anymore. I began a line of questioning from the bed; I tried to console him and offered up several reasons as to why she might not be home.

Since it was summer time, I asked Granddaddy if there were any neighbors outside and he said yes. I asked him if he talked to any of the neighbors to find out if they saw anything. He told me no and he wasn't asking "them no good motherf*rs nothing!" He was adamant that no one would have given him any information if they knew it or not. Boy, did he have a way with words that made you feel all warm and fuzzy inside. NOT!!!

I tried a few more minutes of reasoning with him to no avail. I tried to assure him that perhaps some family members took Grandma to church with them and they just hadn't returned home yet. Then I got off the phone in a panic because I already knew that last scenario hadn't likely occurred. I called my mother to tell her what was going on and she got up immediately, contacted her posse---her aunt, Artra Nell, and cousin, Carmene, who lived near my grandparents to scour the neighborhood looking for her. My mom promised to call me back in an hour, but she didn't. Two hours passed and I was up and waiting on pins and needles for an update. I called her and it was now 1 am and Grandma had not been located.

Eventually, someone was sane enough to go back to the house and look at the Caller ID box. Grandma and I used to get into it over the Caller ID because she kept unplugging it and hiding it around the house. The Caller ID showed that the hospital had phoned the home several times. My mom and her posse went to the hospital to find out what was going on. My mom attempted to pick her up on Sunday and they would not release her until after they spoke with Grandma's regular treating physician. Grandma was held *for observation* until Monday as the hospital was holding her for suspicion of elder abuse. My mom called me extremely upset in a rant as she had to undergo an *interrogation* as she termed it about various marks on Grandma's body.

Grandma was a breast cancer survivor since 1985 having had a mastectomy which required skin grafts from parts of her body. Any other marks on her body could only be explained by her, Granddaddy or God. She was COGIC remember, so she was always in skirts, pantyhose, a full slip or a granny gown. We didn't know what her body looked like since she was still capable of doing her own hygiene. Her release was held up because Grandma couldn't find her upper dentures. She kept asking the hospital staff if they had seen her teeth. The hospital staff was happy to see my mom upon arrival because Grandma's worry about her missing teeth began to cause her distress.

My mom helped search for the missing teeth in a cup, the water pitcher and around the room. They were nowhere to be found. After searching, my mom started to think that the teeth didn't really exist and that Grandma made it up. Dementia does that. Thankfully, the hospital orderly came in to clean and replenish her room. The search was on again and they finally looked under the hospital mattress and found Grandma's *sock*. They should have asked me. I could have told them that; I had plenty of practice.

In lieu of a prosthetic Grandma used sweat socks in a ball to place in her bra. In her old southern tradition, she preferred to keep her precious valuables in her bosom. These valuables included items like money, state ID, senior citizen bus card, social security card and yes even teeth. My mom peeled the layers of the sock back and found her upper denture, a bunch of junk mail credit cards and some New Orleans Mardi Gras beads. Those were the precious valuables she was looking for. My mom says that she burst into laughter seeing her mom's bosom bounty and Grandma got instant relief that she found her teeth.

Grandma was released and thankfully nobody went to jail. Her physician accounted for the scars and gave her medical history. Post discharge instructions communicated to my mom that Grandma required round the clock care since she was incapable of living alone. My mother called me rambling in exasperation of the whole ordeal and said, "People around here needing pills. After the night and day I had --I need a pill! I do, this was a mess! And you know nothing is remembered right? She doesn't remember the paramedics, the fire, being in the hospital or losing her teeth! Alright I got to go!" My mom always

96

says that when she gets frustrated.

Granddaddy was very afraid of the threat of a potential elder abuse hotline call, if she was not adequately supervised. He couldn't make his four-hour errand runs anymore "Cause your Grandmama sick" he would say. My mom, Granddaddy and I met with representatives from the Department on Aging for service options. We discussed adult day care; Grandma declined. We discussed part time care; Grandma declined. We discussed homemaker services. Grandma agreed to that service, a visiting nurse and a podiatrist. The survivor has to agree to services unless you have paperwork to state otherwise, so be prepared for potential refusals to services.

♥ Chapter Reflection ♥

There is so much to reflect on in this chapter, I will begin with the most serious. It is fundamental to understand the degree of risk posed when one leaves individuals with Alzheimer's or other related diseases alone. Alarm system apps and mobile enhanced websites can alert people via texts and notifications when survivors wander. The family's agreement of what to do with items like stoves, microwaves and space heaters that pose additional risks to safety is important. Consider removing or unplugging risky items, removing knobs or setting locking devices to limit access.

Caregiver burnout is real; there should be a line-up of one to two respite providers, for a break. If not, families will run the risk of facing options that they may not be ready for if only they would have worked together. A simple group text or an app like GroupMe keeps interested parties looped in at the same time for more fluid communication. The use of a medical bracelet provides basic information such as the medical condition, allergies, name and an emergency contact number in the event a survivor is lost or disconnected from family for some reason. This might have saved hours of distress and searching if Grandma had her bracelet when this occurred. She got one soon after.

Although my primary focus was on Grandma, Granddaddy clearly needed some love too. We got so lost as a family showering Grandma with the wealth of attention that he felt neglected. He sat in his chair listening like a hawk to every conversation and repeated word for word what was said.

In one of his two-minute heartfelt talks with me, he often said, "Errbody come around here and check on Maggie. Maggie this. Maggie that. Nobody ask about me. Hell, I'm sick too." He went through his litany of ailments to further his point. My heart sank for him as he was absolutely right. We all focused on Grandma's needs because he wasn't as sick as her, we didn't ask about how he

felt, inquired about his doctor's appointments or even washed his clothes. He still drove, paid his own bills, shopped for groceries and *sold a lot of wolf tickets* barking at everybody. It was the bark that kept people away except for me and my kids. Granddaddy always advocated for Jonathan, giving grandfatherly advice telling me *not be so hard on the boy, leave the baby alone* to

saying that N *word heard me talking to him when he was a little older.*

There is so much comfort in those memories of being with him on Sundays because my son, Jonathan, and I would listen to National Public Radio on the

99

way to their house, fuss and argue over the station and then silently listen to whatever was playing. It was the two of us. He did his part talking with Granddaddy who fielded all the family updates from Jon on the sly, since he'd say "No motherf*n body tell me sh*t around here!" I tended to Grandma's care, prepared dinner and completed chores. We stuck to our roles together.

After chit chat time, Granddaddy pulled on his flannel jacket, threw a few commands to Jon and I and walked out the door. He appreciated his little respite get away time; he never said that, but he had such a look of relief to be able to get up and go. It was peaceful and then he would come back nearly when it was time for me to go. Then he'd want me to read some mail, change the volume on his phone or call some bill collector to get more information on Sunday night extending my time beyond the time I intended to stay.

♥ Chapter Reflection ♥

I felt like Granddaddy's personal assistant at times. My mom did too, when she was the live in help. Granddaddy needed love too. I needed those reminders and would do what he asked without question. My mother on the other hand would make it clear to him, "I am not here for you, I am here for mama!" It was funny, but it wasn't; only because I know my mom meant what she said. His delivery in his subtle ask for help sounded like a bunch of complaining and cussing, but if you listened to what he didn't say you would hear that he desired help.

If you reframe the way he operated, it truly was an honor for him to ask you to do those things for him because: 1. He trusted you, 2. He knew you took care of the business and 3. It was his way of letting you know that he needed help, so ordering you to do it took the sting of helplessness aspect of it away. He highly valued education as he had a fifth grade education.

The picture featured in this chapter is a photo of the "cussing man" on Father's Day 2015. It would be his last Father's Day. That day I came at my usual Sunday time for respite. I got Grandma and rolled her onto the porch where we sat for a nice breeze. I didn't greet him and every question he asked I responded with a one-word response. I was very intentional to not acknowledge Father's Day because "it was just another motherf*ing day!" When I took that shot of him I saw how alone he was and felt his sadness as he was remorseful for his actions. He came out on the porch, sent my son to get some popsicles for me after I told him I didn't want any and he sat with us for hours in silence. That was his way of saying I am sorry.

Back story on why I gave him the cold shoulder was from his actions on Mother's Day: Just the month prior, he cussed me out like I was a "ninja" on the street. He was enraged and shook his cane in my face asking me where was his mail because I was "always moving sh*t." I brought Mother's Day to their house---literally with food, drink, plates, cutlery, flowers, gifts, tablecloth and a table. Trust me, it was easier to bring the party to Grandma rather than trying get her out of the house and celebrate. I made do with what I had, so that we could spend quality time with her. My mom, sister, niece, son, uncle and aunt were there too. He almost ruined the mood and he just kept hollering "I don't give a f*ck, it's just another motherf*ing day.

♥ Butt, Thighs and Eyes!   20 ♥

While still in my marriage, I engaged the children to come with me on my Sunday evening visits to check on Grandma and Granddaddy. We did our usual small talk, chit chat session and the kids would show Granddaddy the merits of technology and tried to teach him how to replay sports football highlights on cable television by manipulating the remote control menu. You already know preteens have a lot of energy, take joy in showing adults something we don't know and are way more tech savvy than a seventy something year old can process. That visit was a headache waiting to happen.

For fifteen minutes these little troopers (more like TLM) explained, re-explained, explained again, scrolled through the menu, showed him once, showed him twice and again and again to the point that Granddaddy insisted they stop because he wasn't getting it. He asked them to *write that down*. Thank you Jesus!!!! I was irritated watching this Abbott & Costello train wreck happening, but appreciated the kids willingness to help in whatever way they could. The routine was when I came over Granddaddy would leave and get some free time to himself since it was now his turn to be caretaker. Granddaddy likened this responsibility to being *in prison*: a sentence, restricted with no freedom.

We used to have arguments about who had it worst, him or me. I likened it

102

to showing the scars of your war wounds and comparing whose scar was bigger. He would say, "You had your Grandmama when she was good, but I got her now. She do'n got *worsa*." We'd debate for about ten minutes and would agree to disagree on who had the most responsibility of caring for her. I would avoid the debate as much as I could when Grandma was present because I never knew with certainty if she was picking up what he was putting down. She wasn't talking anymore and it was hard to read whether she was happy or content sometimes and whether she was tuned in to the conversations around her.

From there, I ventured on to another part of the array of cable television options--- the fitness category to explore fitness dance routines. *Why? I don't know because none of us planned to do any exercise.* We found a channel and Grandma sat in her chair bopping her head subtly from side to side tapping her feet to the music. Nicholas and I decided to provide some entertainment; we attempted to do Hip Hop and Bollywood dance moves. I assure you this was not the prettiest scene for two hundred plus pounds of body moving badly in a very heavily heated house with the thermostat set in its customary eighty-degree position year-round. It was fun being silly, at least for me.

I won't even go there about my previous battles with Granddaddy over the heat. On second thought I will; I used to lose my mind over the heat situation and how hard I tried to reason with him to turn it down a little bit (at least when company came). Granddaddy loved to feel heat with all of his southern

Georgian and Floridian roots. He kept the heat setting on HELL. Only Granddaddy could sit up with a shirt, a flannel jacket and some type of hat, long johns and not crack a sweat. It's no wonder they did not dry up in their man made sauna into prunes. It was always too damn hot and we had plenty of arguments about that. Seriously! The homemakers would wear tank tops just to keep from passing out from heat exhaustion. I usually dressed in layers. The minute he hit the door to leave and I saw that blue Buick pull off I would turn the heat down, crack windows, open the front and back door to catch a cross breeze and sometimes run fans.

I digressed, so I tried to goad Grandma into trying a few moves, but she just looked and smiled at me like *not today lady*. I was exhausted from my full five minutes of cardiovascular activity, missteps and all; I decided to take it down a notch and explore some other fitness programs. One program was entitled "Butt, Thighs and Eyes" which looked like something I could've filmed in a back alley with good lighting. The title was catchy so intrigue set in. I flipped to watch what exercise could accomplish exercise for the lower body assets *and* make healthy eyes. The young lady instructing the moves described the actions just as the title stated and directed us, the viewers, to look at her while motioning and pointing to her rear end, her thighs and her eyes.

She busted out into a Tina Turner move thrashing, moving her legs up and down in place at first slow then to lightning speed like a scene from *Flashdance*.

Grandma, the boys and I all exchanged glances at one another and in unison we all cracked up with laughter. Grandma had a hearty laugh and held her mouth to contain herself which made me laugh even more. It was good to see the Grandma I knew show up and laugh at the absurd from time to time. She was still there.

♥ Chapter Reflection ♥

I realized during that visit with the utmost clarity that even in the midst of a time when Grandma could no longer speak she showed us love in her actions by greeting us with the best Grandma hugs and kisses and the fact that she was not able to call our names anymore was absolutely absurd and mind boggling. We could never have prepared ourselves for that even if somebody explained to us that it was going to happen this way.

Her laughter at that absurd exercise segment spoke volumes about those living with Alzheimer's and other related dementias. They may not outwardly communicate in the manner that we are used to, so we have to be vigilant to look for the other ways they speak to us even without a voice. I read somewhere communication is 80% body language and verbal 20% of the time, or something to that effect. This was just one of the many moments when Grandma's spirit pressed past the disease and reminded us that she still internalized things even though she was not able to articulate her feelings and emotions with words anymore. She was still there. Look for it.

She was connected to the music, the comedy of the situation and laughed on cue which was a clear indicator of the lucidity of her awareness. She just couldn't talk. So be mindful of those sensitive conversations and statements you might make in front of them because they still have feelings and experience emotions too. Could you imagine hearing your loved ones talking about you to your face and you could not intervene to stop it? It could be discussions on toileting, hygiene, finances, plans etc. so be mindful of that. And again something about kids and babies always changes the mood.

♥ Catalog Queen 21 ♥

Grandma was affectionately known as Sista Passmore in the circles she traveled and she liked to dress in her Sunday best. Sista Passmore had a couple of closets of clothes because presentation was everything. She had the regular routine of getting her hair done every other week and she came back with this awful lavender purple color – Shimmering something or another. Y'all know what brand I'm talking about. Anyway, Grandma used to order regularly from a certain catalog company and had incurred quite a bill. She had the money, but forgot to make payments on time. She purchased money orders for $20 to pay on her debt at a time when she could have paid for half or all of it.

Grandma was private when it came to paying her bills. She faithfully tithed, paid her own insurance and my uncle's life insurance, took her clothes to the cleaners and made her catalog purchases. After a while, she started receiving notices for delinquent payments and Grandma would get quiet about it and not discuss it with me. I didn't push because after all she was a grown woman still living her life independently, for the most part. I recall I came home and saw new outfits from time to time because she loved when the mail carrier came. I never thought anything about it until I began seeing collection notices and numerous mailings from the same company.

The catalog company refused to process her orders anymore. Grandma took on another identity. She acquired an alias at seventy something years old; she figured out a way to resume ordering her church suits. My mom and I questioned her about her purchases, what was going on and why was she using this other name. She said, "My name *is* Margaret Odessa Williams."

My mother and I looked at each other and burst out laughing. She was adamant that her name was Odessa and her name was not Margaret either. And she argued with conviction that almost gave me pause and made me think perhaps I was wrong. My mom and I both asked Grandma when she acquired a middle name and why was this the first time we had heard of it.

When I later supported my mom as a respite person for her, she loved the company and much like Granddaddy longed for that interaction, my mom gave Grandma her all. We were a team and believed that Grandma deserved the best care we could provide. We did our best to get her out the house and engaged as much as we could. You can find her in many family pictures for a number of family events. Let me get back to the story at hand of *Ms. Margaret!*

She was as we would say back in the day "cold busted" and that little old woman had nerve to catch an attitude as though we had been manipulating her.

108

Both my mom and I had taken up interest in capturing our family roots and this was not something she ever disclosed to us before. Although she did not have a birth certificate at birth, she acquired a delayed one at a much older age and I do not recall ever hearing Margaret or Odessa. This is our exchange:

> Us: *Who called you that?*
>
> Her: *That was what they called me when I was a little girl.*
>
> Us: *Who did?*
>
> Her: *My mama.*
>
> Us: *And who else?*

Although her faculties began to fail her, she was able to recover and resume her ordering under another name, Odessa Williams. My mom straightened the matter out by calling the catalog company and explained the situation. She made regular monthly payments on the bill until it was paid in full. Grandma could no longer order her suits that she could not remember to pay for.

♥ Chapter Reflection ♥

In hindsight, we didn't have to question something deep down that we knew was not true. We caused more angst and upset Grandma unnecessarily and calling the catalog company just as my mom did to explain her medical condition to work something out was appropriate.

This first action would lead to many more arrangements being made to give notice to the bank and other creditors. Thankfully, we secured power of attorney documents at the outset in order to address the finances.

My focus as a caregiver was on meeting the safety and physical needs of my Grandmother that was a wealth of work and not to be taken lightly. I could not be attuned to all the nuances of her physical, emotional/mental, spiritual, financial, health, social and intellectual needs by myself. You are apt to miss some things if you are managing a family, career/job, school, relationship, civic duties and your own health and personal affairs.

*It is absolutely important that you understand YOU CANNOT DO THIS ALONE! You could, but it will be at a cost if you don't garner support and create your village. If you are reading this and you don't have a support system--- **make one**. Albeit a story of my grandmother's fight for independence over ability to manage her finances, there is a much bigger story here and a lesson to be learned.*

The wear and tear on your physical and mental health is real. I wrote this book as a means to help the most important people in the lives of those living with Alzheimer's and other related dementias. My family was a textbook case of what not to do and eventually we got it right. There was more shared responsibility towards the latter part of her life than any other. Some of us stood our ground because the quality of her life was just that important and we made sacrifices. We chose to "keep her at home for as long as we could until we couldn't do it any longer" were the words I have heard my mom utter in the sharing of our story.

We never defined what the any longer looked like and we ended up staying true to our promise until God drafted his angel to go home one October day in 2015. It was heart wrenching and freeing at the same time because Grandma was free. Families will struggle with working it out at home over another facility and whether to medicate or not medicate. I encourage caregivers to try to get input from others and do what is best for you. What is for me may not be for you.

I recall sitting with my mom, dad, son, sister and niece in the waiting room hours after Grandma passed and the image of us together was reassuring of our future. Although my daughter who was away at school, she too could celebrate what love did because we did it together. I rest well every night because we did our best and preserved her dignity through the end.

♥ Don't Ask Me... 22 ♥

I recall one day soon after Granddaddy moved back in with Grandma, I placed a call to them to see how they were doing. Granddaddy and Grandma had a special arrangement: he was at the house daily taking care of household business for a few hours and he would go back home. He checked in, paid bills, cussed out somebody daily, fed the cats, took out the garbage and *"raised sand"* all the time he was there.

He never stopped caring for Grandma though regardless of how they lived apart. It wasn't until much later that I figured out Grandma was a "kept woman," she raised the kids and held a little job every now and then when she was younger, but Granddaddy was the provider. I guess that was how he was raised and he never wanted anybody to question what he did not do for his household.

I knew he had been having a difficult transition settling back in and having to be responsible for her livelihood was completely new to him since she had been such an independent woman. He no longer had the freedom to do and come as he pleased as he had always done as long as I can remember. Back in the day, men worked long hard hours and what he earned he had the right to spend his money how he wanted to as long as he paid the bills. I allowed myself to be the instrument he could use to vent his frustration; trust and believe he was not

112

short on frustration. He accepted his restrictions more readily because the scare of losing her when she was Jane Doe a few hours too long at the local hospital was life changing for him and all of us; you'll find the rest of that story in the chapter entitled *Somebody Don Stole Maggie*.

It became quite evident that caring for his wife of 54 years, at the time, became a real source of frustration for him because he was home 24/7 and acted as Grandma's primary caregiver. On this particular phone call to him, he picked up the phone before finishing a conversation with my grandmother. I said, "Hey Granddaddy!" His opening sentence boomed loudly through the receiver with his signature gruff voice yelling, *"AND DON'T ASK ME THAT NO GOD DAMN MO'! HEEELLO!"* I heard all the frustration in the world squeezed into those two phrases of him clearly not caring who was on the other end of the call. Dementia does that!

He might as well have said, *I'll be damned if she ask me the same thing over and over again.* This was really, really new to him. He had only been home a few weeks and Granddaddy didn't comprehend the magnitude of the ride he was about to take with Grandma for about the next decade. He was buffered from the day to day soap opera because he didn't stay all day waking up to Alzheimer's madness and going asleep to it only to start all over again like *Groundhog Day* with a little different spin daily.

Whatever it was that day she asked him, she'd more than likely asked and asked and asked again. It was just the two of them now. My mom and aunt would eventually move in splitting the week up into four and three. My mom did the four days and I don't know why it didn't switch up, but that would be their arrangement in the middle to end stages of the disease.

When he moved back home for a long time after that, he thought or hoped his companion since adolescence would snap out of it and be the woman he loved again with the big pretty legs and long hair. Whenever he would reminisce about their past, undoubtedly the conversation would always go back to those two things. Grandma was perseverating when her focus got stuck on the one thing that caused her to repeat. *Perseveration* is a term I came to know well and it is just a part of what it is that survivors of Alzheimer's or dementia do.

♥ Chapter Reflection ♥

Granddaddy on any given day was more than likely irritated about something. He had a story to tell coming in the door and you better stop what you were doing to listen. He commanded his attention by dismissing whatever you were doing because it was not as important as what he had to tell you. Period. So add some irritation with a lot of frustration and you got beast to deal with. The frustration one feels as a caregiver is so overwhelming at times that it just doesn't seem real. I found him to be the most hilarious thing on this earth because his bark was way worse than his bite.

*Granddaddy was an older African American male rooted from the south with simple philosophies about life that **if ya educated you should know better** and **if you ain't doin' it a certain way you just plain ole acting stupid** or **when you mess up you never say "I'm sorry" even if you know you are wrong** (at least this rule applied to him). He talked about the way it was supposed to be with something to say about everything except as it relates to this disease. It perplexed him because there was no fixing this. He would talk to anyone who would listen, but it was usually me, "Yo' grandma is getting worsa. It seem like she be doing good and then she go to actin' crazy. She ain't gettin' no betta." It took him about four years to begin to believe she was not faking or that she was intentionally vying for attention. I can't tell you how many times he asked, "You think your Grandmama putting on?" or the number of times which probably numbers in the hundreds of him talking to me about her while she was in his presence. It unnerved me to no end because he had no filter and what he said was his harsh truth.*

*Grandma didn't need to listen to his carrying on. I learned to cut him short, by walking away. He insisted on telling me what my grandma did that day. Just like an old record album skipping, Grandma would respond to him hollering back **"I did not Bobby! Quit tellin' them lies on me Bobby. Shame on you!"** It was a scene I hated being a part of because he didn't understand how damaging his Grandma Report was to her well-being. She was always situated a few feet from him in the living room in their respective spots---she was in her Lazy Boy, he was seated at his medicine table that looked like a shrine to the Pharmacy God.*

115

♥ Going Home   23 ♥

This is most likely the hardest chapter of them all that I had to construct. Most chapters were written many years ago, while this one is freshly written since my grandparents have both transitioned home. I had always envisioned that there would be a photo of my grandmother holding a copy of this book in hand and my granddaddy smiling a toothless smile bragging to everyone who could hear about his *college educated* granddaughter's book. I can only hold on to what their spirit would say and revel in their love for me, hoping it is pleasing to them and a job well done in sharing their story so that it might be of benefit to someone else.

What's Funny About Dementia? was to have been originally published in 2009. Life happened. Then my world came crashing down when both my grandparents transitioned in October 2015; first Grandma and then two weeks later Granddaddy died on Halloween. I was already in a season of grief and experienced so much death at one time, I felt like I was *going through the motions* of living. Grief had been a foreign thing to me and I would often hand those referrals off to my peers in the counseling field, but now my personal experience has afforded me some unwanted education on the subject. My motivation waned for a moment and came back fiercely as I celebrate their transition home because their imprint lingers.

This book was supposed to have been my first that I authored, but time got away from me. I lost two years after their death grieving those two unexpected losses and that of my best friend two months prior. Too much, too soon in such a short time frame jettisoned me to live *a new normal* consisting of numbness and a loss of joy. It was too painful to write. I had been unscathed by deaths so close to me for a long time and it was just too devastating to finish sooner. I've started another book on the subject of grief as a result of this life changing experience that I could not fully conceptualize until I went through it myself both feet in. Death has loyalty to nothing other than the inevitable.

Finishing this book meant changing the stories from present tense to past tense because they are no longer here. The many memories of them are close to my heart and I have no regrets about my relationships with them both because I know they loved me as much as I loved them all of my life. I can say with certainty that I helped to prolong their life just a little bit with God's grace and His compassion.

The longer they lived, the more I realized that you couldn't sweat the small stuff; living life angry and holding grudges against those who refused to help or offer an encouraging word did nothing for my spirit. This would prove to be an even harder pitch to sell to my mom who would probably characterize her experience as a "hellish" five years trying to understand why family didn't support Grandma's care more than they did. I did my best; I nor anyone else can fault me for trying to make sure their end of life was filled with love, integrity, care and concern for their wellbeing.

I no longer joke with my kids to *shoot me when I get this bad* if an Alzheimer's diagnosis is to be my fate referring to those frustrating moments in caregiving when I felt like I carried the weight of the universe upon my shoulders. If my health declines and dementia settles in, my only ask is that my children and family remember it is still me on the inside. I pray that you find a way to get others to share in the work with you or let the spirit move them out the way, so as to not be a distraction for the important work at hand.

♥ Chapter Reflection ♥

The sum of it: Mr. Alzheimer's enslaved my grandfather to his will. He never conceptualized that his wife could be sick, take medicine and still get "worsa." Yes, he said, "worsa." Imagine if your companion just stopped talking one day---forever! She'd never cook a meal again. No more beans, collard greens and her all-star turkey wings and dressing. She would be directed when to use the restroom, when to get up and when to lie down.

As the provider and protector Granddaddy couldn't fix her, fix it or fix their new way of being. The only thing he could do was wish a mother%$@@ would come in his house and tell him what he could and could not do. All he had was his castle. But Mr. was stronger than

Granddaddy. Mr. had been in the game a long time and had staying power.

Mr. took Granddaddy's wife right from under him and took over. He dominated his wife's sleep, quashed her joy and love of church. He made her a mute, took away "her big pretty legs" and left Granddaddy to his own seventy-plus-year old imagination of what she needed and desired. No more streets. No more leisure. Every day was work and every night was pain.

Granddaddy would tell everyone who would listen that his caregiving experience was like he was in prison. All attention was on her and not on him. No wonder when visitors came to see Grandma, they became Granddaddy's visitors. He felt alone and needed to be shown love too!

He nipped his toe one summer and never said a word about the infection that had been eating away at his foot. When she went into the hospital, he asked, "Your Grandmama ain't doing so good, huh?" He needed no answer, but just had to say it aloud. It was then he decided he would go into the hospital for care of his foot, only after knowing she was likely going home and was finally going to be alright.

Granddaddy did not leave this earth before her because that is not what protectors and providers do. When Grandma died a part of him died too. No last words. No sweet caresses. No hug good bye. Granddaddy died two weeks later without his companion of 64 yrs. Love won!

Mr. will never beat love. Hold fast to your survivors and never stop loving them regardless of their ability. They need you to help fight the battle with Mr. and anything that would get in the way of living and be their advocate.

Never put off for tomorrow what you could do today because time waits for no one. Live without regrets and learn to forgive those around you who could do more to help, but don't. Center your thoughts on how you can be the best helper you can be and let God take care of the rest. The Serenity Prayer teaches you to "accept the things you cannot change and the wisdom to know the difference when you can't."

♥ Acknowledgements ♥

If it were not for God, who carried me through the roughest of times allowing me to find meaning in my journey while gifting me with the blessing of humility--- where would I be, where would I be? My steps were ordered with purpose. I am so grateful to my mother, *Barbara*, whom I relied upon when I felt like my life was a living hell during my turn as the sole caregiver. My friends and colleagues (*Lisa Timberlake and Wanda Williams*) allowed me to debrief my experiences as they were my therapy during the years my health, mind and spirit were impacted by the toll of caregiving in the midst of all the other things life brings. *Robert Colucci*, my cube mate, swapped stories with me and was my saving grace. We laughed until tears streamed from our eyes as we both shared the role of being the "responsible family member" in our respective caregiver roles. My then husband, *Dwayne*, never complained about my respite activities and accompanied me at times showing patience and understanding. Huge thanks are extended to the *National Association of Black Social Workers* and the local *Chicago Chapter* for providing me with the platform to speak into existence my public promise to give voice to the illness that changed our lives. Finally, thank you to the families across the world who cry out time and time again wishing the disease would reverse itself and give us back the people we once knew. If we watch and listen long enough we will always know they are still here as their true essence never leaves. Special thanks to Dr. Carlton-LeNay, Dr. Knight, Dr. Williams and Debbie Smith-Mack for their reviews! Thank you Dr. Obari Cartman for the opening words in the Foreword.

♥ Feedback Request ♥

Your feedback is immensely appreciated on this book project. Please leave your reviews, comments or share your experience with Dementia on:

Facebook: Jataun Rollins, Author & Speaker

Instagram: jataunspeaks

Twitter: JataunR

Email at: jataunrollinsauthor@gmail.com

You can also add #WFADLAUGH

to your posts, so I keep track of them.

God bless you!

Jataun

♥ Appendix ♥

Caregiver Self-Care Activities

Ephesians 6:13 *Therefore put on the full armor of God, so that when the day of evil comes you may be able to stand your ground and after you have done everything to stand. (NIV)*

Grandma would be pleased that I went back to my roots and included words of scripture to bring it back to basics; after all it was her *bread and butter.* I have included some activities that the caregiver or the spouse/partner can engage in to take care of their own respective needs to sustain healthy well-being. In the course of supporting my grandparents through our family's battle with Alzheimer's, many people either indicated humor, spirituality or a combination of both kept them sane.

Some people give it up to God, pray about their situation, journal, confide in friends and family, see a therapist or a blend of measures to walk them through a significant event that is having a deleterious impact on their quality of life. It is my hope that you be encouraged to live life more fully within your purpose and passion, so as to not lose yourself in the midst of caregiving. Explore your options and choose.

Self-Care Suggestions:

✓ Purchase a journal to track your journey through your caretaking experience.

✓ Make a purchase of a special pen for your writings.

✓ Set aside a day, time and place to work through your self-care exercises.

✓ A soothing caffeine-free tea or your favorite beverage in your special mug or cup may help you relax.

✓ Seek additional support with a trusted friend, a local therapist/counselor, or a clergy person at a faith based institution.

Complete the following activities for self-actualization, defined as maximizing your potential and doing the best that you are capable of doing.[7] It will help you distress those moments in your life when you feel overwhelmed. The role of the caregiver is critical to the survivor, but more importantly to self or the caregiver will be of no value if they are burnt out. This book is focused on the wellness of the caregiver and I implore you to select what works for you and make it a part of your routine.

[7]https://www.huffingtonpost.com/david-sze/maslow-the-12-characteris_b_7836836.html
Retrieved February 13, 2008

Psalm 107:8 *Let them give thanks to the Lord for his unfailing love and His wonderful deeds for mankind... (NIV)*

Mindful Matters: Sit quietly for five minutes, meditate in the moment, think about your best self, reflect on the goodness of God and any time God has carried you through a valley. Push all other thoughts and distractions aside that surface and continue to be in the moment of channeling your best self. Keep bringing your mind back to the meditation at hand when your thoughts stray away. Be humbled in spirit and thank God for being a forgiving God.

Psalm 118:24 This is the day that the Lord has made; let us rejoice and be glad in it. (NIV)

Inner Peace Actualized: Describe what inner peace looks like to you. Find 3-5 pictures of you during a time in your life that you can recall when you felt inner peace. Write the moments of your life that you would've characterized as inner peace.

Jeremiah 29:11 *For I know the plans I have for you declares the Lord, "plans to prosper you and not to harm you, plans to give you hope and future." (NIV)*

Hold On To Your Dreams: Take five minutes of your time and brainstorm all the things you can remember that you desired or forecasted as a child or in your youth that you would be or do as an adult. (i.e. travel the world, be President of the United States, sing in a choir, drive a Cadillac, own your own business, etc.)

Psalm 37:5 *Commit thy way unto the Lord; Trust also in Him; and He shall bring it to pass. (NIV)*

Make Meaning of the Lesson(s): Take time to reflect on what you are experiencing. What meaning do you make of these experiences? What is God telling you? Have you ever been broken? If so, did you rebuild? What lesson that came from that experience?

James 3:18 Peacemakers who sow in peace reap a harvest of righteousness. (NIV)

Olive Branch: List at least two people who you desire forgiveness from even if it is yourself (if applicable). Write a note card or a letter to them and frame your forgiveness focusing on what behavior you engaged in on your behalf.

15 Point Dementia Caregiver Assessment

These fifteen points are significant in assessment of the dementia caregiver for consideration of their capacity to provide care, understand their current support system and identify factors that might impact care. This assessment will enable the professional to understand the caregiver's resources, help determine their physical stamina to provide care, ascertain the dementia caregiver's perception of this experience and learn what coping mechanisms they have in reserve to handle stress.

My position is that the intricacies of what the caregiver brings to the table are sometimes overlooked. This is a great opportunity to get an idea of what is going on in the caregiver's life to offer local resources or determine whether or how their support system needs to expand outside of immediate and extended family members.

1. Age

2. Gender

3. Literacy

4. Resourcefulness

5. Support system

6. Hobbies/Interests

7. Access to transportation

8. Other caretaking responsibilities

9. Level of religiosity or spirituality

10. Locale: rural or urban community

11. Civic and volunteer responsibilities

12. General Health: physical and emotional

13. Economic Stability: employment status and financial resources

14. Proficiency with computers, smart phones and social media platforms

15. Quality of the pre-morbid relationship with the individual who has Alzheimer's or other dementia

Activities to Engage Survivors of Alzheimer's and Other Dementias

These activities below enable family/friends ways to engage with survivors to combat boredom, strengthen familial bonds, help children & teens to engage with survivors, distract and stimulate the survivor's mind.[8] Activities can break up the monotony of the day, provide normalcy, a form of exercise, opportunities to laugh.

Balloon Volleyball

You can get a pack of oversized balloons from your local dollar store and use them as a beach ball. This activity is kid friendly in that it is fun for them and provides a form of exercise for the survivor. It enables young children to engage with the survivor to aid in bonding.

Chair Bowl

You can use water bottles in a ten pin formation and a tennis ball or any ball with a little weight to it or go to your local big box store and by a children's set of bowling pins. It is another way to engage the survivor in exercise and aid in intergenerational bonding.

Photo Scrapbook

Depending on the stage of the disease, this photo scrapbook allows the survivor to engage in visual memories that may prompt conversation or stories. A photo scrapbook also can help the survivor recognize family and friends, especially those who visit often.

[8]Bazan-Salazar, E. Alzheimer's Activities That Stimulate the Mind. New York: McGraw-Hill, 2005.

130

BALLOON VOLLEYBALL	CHAIR BOWL
	Image: Creative Dish
PHOTO SCRAPBOOK	CHILDREN'S BOOK READ
GARDEN	MEAL PREPARATION
image: backyardriches.com	
CHAIR DANCE	WASTEBASKET BASKETBALL
SING NURSERY RHYMES	YOGA
	Image: Yoga for 'Every Body'

131

Children's Book Read (Big Print)

Engage the survivor in reading to a child to help stimulate the mind and aid in intergeneration bonding with meaningful activity that will provide lasting memories of engagement with their family member. Pictures of these precious moments are priceless.

Garden

Nadine Clark-Harris, a garden enthusiast in Chicago, consults about the healing benefits and life lessons of gardening as a means of enhancing well-being. Studies indicate the physical activity of hoeing, pulling weeds, watering plants, etc. burn calories. Tending a garden enhances the likelihood of eating more healthier nutrient options leading to better health outcomes. Even NASA endorses the benefits of gardening highlighting the impact to sensory stimulation of the visual, tactile, olfactory and salivary stimulation which counters sensory monotony.[9]

Meal Prep

The survivor can be engaged in daily meal prep: making sandwiches, picking greens, cracking and beating eggs, shuck corn, snap peas, stir cornbread, make punch/Kool-Aid, butter bread. They may or may not be able to cook meals, so this is one way to keep the survivor engaged with less idle time.

---

[9]NASA/Johnson Space Center. (2016, January 21). Zinnias from space! NASA studies the multiple benefits of gardening. *ScienceDaily*. Retrieved February 18, 2018 from www.sciencedaily.com/releases/2016/01/160121121528.htm

Chair Dance

Play music from different eras that the survivor might connect with and provide them with a scarf, tie, flag or a piece of material for them to wave. It provides movement of the upper body sitting without tiring them out.

Wastebasket Basketball

Crumple paper and use a wastebasket for a ball and hoop. It provides range of motion of the arms and is a very cheap way to engage the survivor in exercise.

Sing Nursery Rhymes

Nursery Rhymes are attached to long memory and singing as they are an effortless task where family and friends can sing-a-long to tunes like: Twinkle, Twinkle Little Star, Patty Cake, Old Mary Mack, Rockin' Robin, Old King Cole, Yankee Doodle Dandy and any cultural/regional song you may know. Helping the survivor to be engaged with human interaction is critical.

Yoga

The practice of yoga, dating back as far as five thousand years has scientific backing of its effectiveness in helping to reduce atrophy of the hippocampus and decreases cortisol levels helping to slow the progression of Alzheimer's.[10] Relaxation and meditation at least 2 to 3 times a week is hugely beneficial for the survivor and the caretaker.

[10]https://www.alzheimers.net/2013-11-25/how-meditation-can-slow-alzheimers/

Retrieved February 18, 2018

35 Question Checklist of Behavioral Changes

to Screen for Alzheimer's

Participants should only circle 'yes' if their behaviour has been present for **at least six**

months and is unusual to them. Severity is then measured on a scale from one to three,

with **three being the most dramatic change of symptoms and one the least.**

This domain describes *interest, motivation, and drive*

Has the person lost interest in friends, family, or home activities? Y N 1 2 3

Does the person lack curiosity in topics that would usually have attracted her/his

interest? Y N 1 2 3

Has the person become less spontaneous and active for example, is she/he less likely to

initiate or maintain conversation? Y N 1 2 3

Has the person lost the motivation to act on their obligations or interests? Y N 1 2 3

Is the person less affectionate and/or lacking in emotions when compared to her/his

usual self? Y N 1 2 3

Does she/he no longer care about anything? Y N 1 2 3

This domain describes *mood or anxiety symptoms*

Has the person developed sadness or appear to be in low spirits? Does he/she have

episodes of tearfulness? Y N 1 2 3

Has the person become less able to experience pleasure? Y N 1 2 3

Has the person become discouraged about their future or feel that she/he is a failure?
Y N 1 2 3

Does the person view herself/himself as a burden to family? Y N 1 2 3

Has the person become more anxious or worried about things that are routine (e.g. events, visits, etc.)? Y N 1 2 3

Does the person feel very tense, having developed an inability to relax, or shakiness, or symptoms of panic? Y N 1 2 3

This domain describes the *ability to delay gratification and control behavior, impulses, oral intake and/or changes in reward*

Has the person become agitated, aggressive, irritable, or temperamental? Y N 1 2 3

Has she/he become unreasonably or uncharacteristically argumentative? Y N 1 2 3

Has the person become more impulsive, seeming to act without considering things?
Y N 1 2 3

Does the person display sexually disinhibited or intrusive behaviour, such as touching (themselves/others), hugging, groping, etc., in a manner that is out of character or may cause offence? Y N 1 2 3

Has the person become more easily frustrated or impatient? Does she/he have troubles coping with delays, or waiting for events or for their turn? Y N 1 2 3

Does the person display a new recklessness or lack of judgement when driving (e.g. speeding, erratic swerving, abrupt lane changes, etc.)? Y N 1 2 3

135

Has the person become more stubborn or rigid, i.e., uncharacteristically insistent on having their way, or unwilling/unable to see/hear other views? Y N 1 2 3

Is there a change in eating behaviors (e.g., overeating, cramming the mouth, insistent on eating only specific foods, or eating the food in exactly the same order)? Y N 1 2 3

Does the person no longer find food tasteful or enjoyable? Are they eating less? Y N 1 2 3

Does the person hoard objects when she/he did not do so before? Y N 1 2 3

Has the person developed simple repetitive behaviors or compulsions? Y N 1 2 3

Has the person recently developed trouble regulating smoking, alcohol, drug intake or gambling, or started shoplifting? Y N 1 2 3

This domain describes following *societal norms and having social graces, tact, and empathy*

Has the person become less concerned about how her/his words or actions affect others? Has she/he become insensitive to others feelings? Y N 1 2 3

Has the person started talking openly about very personal or private matters not usually discussed in public? Y N 1 2 3

Does the person say rude or crude things or make lewd sexual remarks that she/he would not have said before? Y N 1 2 3

Does the person seem to lack the social judgement she/he previously had about what to say or how to behave in public or private? Y N 1 2 3

Does the person now talk to strangers as if familiar, or intrude on their activities? Y N 1 2 3

This domain describes *strongly held beliefs and sensory experiences*

Has the person developed beliefs that they are in danger, or that others are planning to harm them or steal their belongings? Y N 1 2 3

Has the person developed suspiciousness about the intentions or motives of other people? Y N 1 2 3

Does she/he have unrealistic beliefs about her/his power, wealth or skills? Y N 1 2 3

Does the person describe hearing voices or does she/he talk to imaginary people or spirits? Y N 1 2 3

Does the person report or complain about, or act as if seeing things (e.g. people, animals or insects) that are not there, i.e., that are imaginary to others? Y N 1 2 3[11]

---

[11]http://www.dailymail.co.uk/health/article-3714806/Will-Alzheimer-s-Answer-questions-Checklist-shows-   symptoms-disease-memory-loss.html#ixzz56j2TrKMq retrieved February 10, 2018.

Twelve Steps to Help Manage
Alzheimer's and Other Related Diseases

1. Upon diagnosis, *consider a second opinion to help affirm diagnosis of the disease and explore all your options.* Not accepting the reality of this new life presents the danger of delaying decision making processes that will set forth in motion and leaves your loved one without the supportive services that they need.

2. *Recognize this is not a task that has to be completed alone* nor should you try to carry the weight by yourself. Organizations like the Alzheimer's Association can direct you to resources in your area. There are studies being done around the world at hospitals and universities.

3. *Develop a core group of family or friends to become caretakers* and have a family meeting at the outset working out a plan for who will do what, when and how often. Preserve the dignity of the individual living with Alzheimer's and have conversations about limitations and struggles outside of their presence.

4. *Contact your local government for possible resources.* Look up the Department of Aging in your area at the city and state level. They can direct you to in home services and other options.

5. If you have the resources, *contact an attorney who will be able to assist you with financial affairs or a local legal law clinic.* The sooner, the better as it will be difficult to legitimize the legality of agreements and legal documents if the person with dementia is deemed incapable of making decisions for themselves.

6. *Develop a plan of care for yourself* to create a reserve of energy, stamina and perseverance to do battle. Exercise, keep your medical appointments and follow through, have lunch out, attend church or just get out of the house for the sake of your own physical and mental well-being.

7. *Be observant of the needs of your loved one* in order to ensure that any supportive sources are aware of the current level of functioning and follow up is made to an appropriate source.

8. *Develop a system* for keeping appointments and a more consistent routine that are central to all those involved to provide transparency and continuity of care.

9. *Consider joining a support group* or find someone you can confide in to allow you the opportunity to vent your frustrations. Don't be afraid to share with your friends and family. The weight of this is too much to bear alone. You can find a group on the web, social media.

10. *Recognize your limits and be mindful of when you begin to feel overwhelmed or sad* more times than not. Don't neglect your time alone as it is essential to your emotional, spiritual and physical balance in order to be well and of assistance to those you care for and your own family.

11. *Explore all your options* available to you and *make decisions based on feasibility.* If you find it isn't working, then rework it until it works for you.

12. *Hold close to the good moments* when you are able to laugh, smile and engage in meaningful conversation with the person whom you are caring for. These will be the very moments to carry you through your journey. Your journey won't be like any other and it is important that you come out of it well.

Glossary: Clinical Language Made Plain

Action Plan: A plan outlining what action is needed, who will do what, in what timeframe and if the goal is achieved

Assess: Get a picture of what is going on

Assessment: More formally use a questionnaire, survey or a tool to understand your experiences or that of the survivor

Counseling/Therapy: talk about some of the things going on in life; vent problems

Day Care/Program: A senior program that provides activities for aging individuals to stay engaged and designed to help with social interaction

Familial AD: more than one family member impacted by Alzheimer's disease

Homemaker: A helper that assists with housekeeping, organizing, accompanying clients for medical appointments and cooking

Perseveration: Stuck on a thought or phrase that is repeated often

Reframe: Find the light in every situation and reshape into a positive thought

Religious:	Formal practice of religion attending worship service
Respite:	A period of time that offers a break or get away time
Self-care:	Taking care of one's self doing things that tend to physical, medical, social and emotional well-being that bring joy, replenish or energize
Spirituality:	A belief in a higher power, entity or being
Sporadic AD:	one member of the family impacted by Alzheimer's disease
Staffing:	A meeting usually with professionals and family to discuss diagnosis or issues that are pertinent to the care and health of the survivor
Sundown:	late or night time confusion, anxiety and irritation
Support System:	A unit of support that may come from family, friends, peers, church members, neighbors, colleagues and institutions

Bibliography/Resources

Bazan-Salazar, E. (2005). *Alzheimer's Activities That Stimulate the Mind*. New York: McGraw Hill.

Callone, P. R. (2006). *A Caregiver's Guide to Alzheimer's disease: 300 Tips for Making Life Easier*. New York, New York: Demos Medical Publishing.

Costing, J. K. (2003). *Learning to Speak Alzheimer's: A Groundbreaking Approach for Everyone Dealing with the Disease*. New York, New York: Houghton Mifflin.

Devi, G. (2017). *The Spectrum of Hope: An Optimistic and New Approach to Alzheimer's Disease and Other Dementias*. New York, New York :Workman Publishing.

Gallagher-Thompson, D., Naythons, M. & Castleman, M. *There's Still a Person in There: The Complete Guide to Treating and Coping with Alzheimer's*. New York, New York: Putnam House.

Gray-Davison, F. (1999). *The Alzheimer's Sourcebook for Caregivers: A Practical Guide for Getting Through the Day*. Los Angeles, CA: Lowell House.

Knutson, L. D. (2007). *Compassionate Caregiving: Practical Help & Spiritual Encouragement*. Bloomington, MN: Bethany House.

Kuhn, D. (2003). *Alzheimer's Early Stages First Steps for Family, Friends and Caregivers*. Alameda, CA: Hunter House.

Mace, N. L. (1981). *The 36-hour day: a Family Guide To Caring For Persons With Alzheimer's Disease, Related Dementing Illnesses, And Memory Loss In Later Life*. Baltimore: Johns Hopkins University Press.

Ornstein, R. & Sobel, D. (1989). *Healthy Pleasures*. Reading, MA: Perseus Books.

Memoirs

Geist, M. E. (2008). *Measure of the Heart: A Father's Alzheimer's, A Daughter's Return*. New York, New York: Springboard Press.

Kessler, L. (2007). *Finding Life in the Land of Alzheimer's: One Daughter's Hopeful Story*. New York, New York: Penguin.

McClure, P. (2015). *Losing a Hero to Alzheimer's: The Story of Pearl*. Bloomington, IN: Westbow Press.

Owens, V. S. (2007). *Caring for Mother: A Daughter's Long Goodbye*. Louisville, KY: John Knox Press.

Perry-Osler, A. (2012). *Learning to Love Olivia*. Lansing, IL: Lifelines Publishing.

Veney, L. (2013). *Being My Mom's Mom*. West Conshohocken, PA: Infinity.

Journal Articles

Heinemann, T. (2009). Managing unavoidable conflicts in caretaking of the elderly: Humor as a mitigating resource. *International Journal of the Sociology of Language*. 200, 103-127.

Lefcourt, H., & Thomas, S. (1998). Humor and Stress revisited. In W. Ruch (Ed.). The Sense of humor: Explorations of a personality characteristic (pp. 179-202). Berlin: Mouton de Gruyter.

Martin, R. A. (2007). The Psychology of Humor: An Integrative Approach. Burlington: Elsevier.

Parrish, M., Laughing your way to peace of mind: How a little humor helps caregivers survive. *Clinical Social Work Journal*. 27, 203-211.

Thorson J., Powell, F., Sarmany-Schuller, I., Hampes, W. (1997). *Psychological Health and Sense of Humor*. Journal of Clinical Psychology. 53, 605-619.

Goldman, J. S., Hahn, S. E., Williamson Catania, J. et al: "Genetic Counseling and Testing for Alzheimer Disease: Joint Practice Guidelines of the American College of Medical Genetics and the National Society of Genetic Counselors." Genetics in Medicine Volume 13(6): *pages 597-605, June 2011.*

Newspaper Articles

Daly, J. (2015, June 3). Alzheimer's: a tough enemy. *Chicago Tribune*, p 1.

Mars, N. (2015, June 3). Dance therapy brings out the unspeakable. *Chicago Tribune*, p 2.

Sadick, B. (2015, June 3). Alzheimer's researcher calls for more volunteers. *Chicago Tribune*, p 2.

Stevens, H. (2015, June 3). Americans view elderly care as duty of females. *Chicago Tribune*, p 1.

Noland, S. (2017, April 26-May 2). The Black Caregiver Crisis. *Chicago Defender*, pp 2,3.

Internet Sources

http://www.alz.org/documents/national/World_Alzheimer_Report_2010_Summary(1).pdf Retrieved October 28, 2011

http://www.hbo.com/alzheimers/grandpa-do-you-know-who-i-am.html Retrieved October 28, 2011

http://www.beliefnet.com/Health/2008/09/Guide-to-Caring-for-a Parent-with-Alzheimer's.aspx3ixzzlbCXqV07E Retrieved October 28, 2011

https://www.brightfocus.org/alzheimers/article/burden-alzheimers-disease-african-americans Retrieved February 04, 2018

https://www.alz.org/national/documents/report_africanamericanssilentepidemic.pdf
Retrieved February 4, 2018

http://www.nia.nih.gov/health/common -questions-about-partcipating-alzheimers-and-related-dementias-research Retrieved February 4, 2018

https://www.aarp.org/home-family/caregiving/info-2017/being-my-moms-caregiver-saved-me.html Retrieved February 26, 2018

https://www.nia.nih.gov/health/common-questions-about-participating-alzheimers-and-related-dementias-research Retrieved February 04, 2018

https://www.alz.org/national/documents/report_africanamericanssilentepidemic.pdf
Retrieved February 04, 2018

https://www.brightfocus.org/alzheimers/article/burden-alzheimers-disease-african-americans Retrieved February 04, 2018

Finding Studies

Mount Sinai Alzheimer's Disease Research Center www.mssm.edu.adrc 212.241.8321

Alzheimer's Association www.alz.org   800.272.3900

Alzheimer's Disease Education and Referral Center www.alzheimers.org 800.438.4380

National Institutes of Health Clinical Trials www.clinicaltrials.gov

https://trialmatch.alz.org/find-clinical-trials/alz#login